Beyond The Battlefield

Beyond the Battlefield

A Guide to Conquering Life's Challenges

Christopher Lee

©2024 All Rights Reserved. No portion of this book may be reproduced, stored in a retrieval system, or transmitted in any form or by any means—electronic, mechanical, photocopy, recording, scanning, or other—except for brief quotations in critical reviews or articles without the prior permission of the author.

Published by Game Changer Publishing

Paperback ISBN: 978-1-964811-84-0
Hardcover ISBN: 978-1-964811-04-8
Digital: ISBN: 978-1-964811-05-5

www.GameChangerPublishing.com

Read This First

Just to say thanks for buying and reading *Beyond the Battlefield*, I would like to give you a free workbook to use. No strings attached! Scan the code below to download your copy.

Scan the QR Code Here:

Beyond The Battlefield

A Guide to Conquering Life's Challenges

Christopher Lee

www.GameChangerPublishing.com

Table of Contents

Introduction 1

Chapter 1 – It's All Up to You 5

Chapter 2 – Who the Hell Are You? 23

Chapter 3 – Become the Most Interesting Person You Know 41

Chapter 4 – You Should Be the Calmest One in the Room 55

Chapter 5 – "Show Me Your Friends and I'll Show You Your Future" 69

Chapter 6 – Look Good Naked and Be Hard to Kill 83

Chapter 7 – Wealth Doesn't Happen by Accident 99

Chapter 8 – How to Make It Happen 113

Conclusion 131

Additional Reading 135

Introduction

Full disclosure: I rarely read introductions to books. It's a bad habit I'm sure I picked up in college and comes from my desire to jump into the material. I want to get rolling and dig into the stuff that'll change my life or offer insight into progressing forward or improving. So, I almost feel like I'm betraying my values in writing this introduction, but for those wanting to know what this book is about, I'll offer a little glimpse into what to expect moving forward.

This isn't an autobiography but rather my philosophy on what it takes to achieve all you want in life. The following pages are filled with thoughts derived from my personal experience on what it takes to achieve greatness in your own life, whatever greatness looks like to you. As I continue to grow and move on my own journey, I anticipate my philosophy will continue to evolve.

A word of warning: I spent ten years in the Army, and as a result, my filter is a little loose. So, if you're offended by swearing, I apologize in advance… not for my swearing, but for the state of your delicate psyche. Don't lose the message because of a few words written by an adult to an audience of adults. Okay, enough of that.

Chapter 1 will discuss who is responsible for your current state in life and who is responsible for the future direction of your life. Spoiler alert—it's *you*. Additionally, I will touch on the most precious commodity humans have, and it's definitely not money. It's time. Time is the one thing we can never earn more of. Are you capitalizing on the opportunities given to you every day?

Chapter 2 will dig into the first step you need to take to achieve all you desire. Goals are great, but figuring out the kind of person you want to be will ultimately trump any goal you set for yourself. Your identity is the value system upon which your life is—and will be—built. I lay out steps and exercises to ensure that your foundation is rock solid.

Chapter 3 is all about becoming a more interesting person. And why should you care about that? Because becoming more interesting requires work and ensures you're chasing after things you're passionate about. The second- and third-order effects include being better able to connect with the people in your life and learning skills that make you more useful to your tribe, community, and the world.

Chapter 4 teaches you the importance of remaining calm. Staying calm isn't necessary in times of peace, but it is in times of chaos. I'll give you some techniques, share my perspective on what it means to be in complete control of one's emotions, and explain how that control leads to greater freedom and growth as an individual.

Chapter 5 will discuss the importance of surrounding oneself with high-caliber people. Navigating life completely alone is not only suboptimal but also impossible. The people you surround yourself with direct the trajectory of your life in a bigger way than you may think or want, but it is what it is. I provide simple questions to ask yourself when creating a community of consequences.

Chapter 6 will talk about the importance of staying healthy. Being physically fit is one of the fastest ways to positively affect the direction of your life. A healthy body is a testament to one's daily habits, actions, and level of discipline, and these three things carry over into all areas of life. A fit body is an external representation of one's internal strength.

Chapter 7 will talk about money. Money is one of those things that isn't discussed much among friends, and I don't know why. It's an important part of life, and one's relationship with money heavily influences the emotions involved when interacting with it and thinking about it. I include several exercises to dig into the relationship you have with money and see whether or not it can be improved.

Chapter 8 tells you how to put it all together. I'm a firm believer that it's pretty difficult to compartmentalize one's life because all areas are connected. This final chapter ties all the others together with a practical step-by-step plan to make sure you're not neglecting any area of your life but are thriving in all areas. Slow and steady is the name of the game, so if you're too impatient to think and plan long-term for your life, you might struggle with this philosophy. That's okay, though—we'll get through it together.

In addition to the exercises provided throughout this book, I've included some book titles at the end of each chapter. I recommend these books because they've been foundational in my own journey and have inspired me to continue to chase excellence. You can find a more exhaustive list of recommended readings at the end of this book. I hope you enjoy it.

CHAPTER 1

It's All Up to You

"Good people will do what they find honorable to do, even if it requires hard work; they'll do it even if it causes them injury; they'll do it even if it will bring danger. Again, they won't do what they find base, even if it brings wealth, pleasure, or power. Nothing will deter them from what is honorable, and nothing will lure them into what is base."

–Seneca, Moral Letters, 76.18[1]

We need to get something straight. And this will make some of you uncomfortable and even piss some of you off, but it needs to be said: The trajectory of your life is entirely your responsibility. I'll say it again another way—you are 100 percent responsible for how your life turns out. Some of you read that and got motivated. And some of you read it and immediately started arguing with me (which is silly because you're reading a book, and I'm not actually there). There's a great deal in this life that we have zero control over. Horrible things happen. I'm not diminishing whatever circumstances you may have experienced. I'm reminding you that you have control over how you respond to the life you're living. If you're not living the life you want, there are probably multiple reasons for it, but the biggest one can be found in the mirror. "Okay, Chris, fine," you might say. "I accept responsibility for my

---

[1] Holiday, Ryan, and Stephen Hanselman, *The Daily Stoic: 366 Meditations on Wisdom, Perseverance, and the Art of Living*, 202.

life. Now what?" I'm glad you asked. There are several factors you should start looking at if you want to make a serious change in your life. The first one is motivation.

The Carrot or the Stick

I've found that most people won't choose to grow until the fear of staying the same is greater than the fear of changing. Some people are motivated by a prize, while others are motivated by pain. Pain, or the fear of pain, can be an excellent driver for one's success.

But at what point do you look at yourself in the mirror and say, "Damn, I'm gross. I need to make a change." Or look at your bank account balance after drinking away your boredom over the weekend and wonder why you can't ever seem to get ahead. These intentional reality checks and moments of self-reflection are important and should be done regularly.

When things are painful or uncomfortable, it's easy to find the motivation to change. However, the most difficult time to change is when you're comfortable—your bills are paid on time, you take a vacation once a year, and you have food on your table. Maybe your health and level of fitness are "good enough." Or you're totally okay with having never picked up a book since high school. There's really no incentive to change or grow when you're in a position like this. So why would anyone want to move from there? You might say to yourself, "I do my job well, so I don't need to continue to learn new things."

But perhaps you should ask yourself some questions. What do you consider successful? What level of financial security works best for you? What level of fitness is acceptable to you? How smart do you really want to be? If the scenario I described above is "good enough," then congratulations—you can probably stop reading this book now. The words written here are aimed at those of you who want to see how far they can go as an individual. How far can one pursue excellence before hitting the ceiling? The goal of this book is to encourage you not to create a false ceiling for yourself.

People will accuse you of being greedy for pursuing great wealth, vain for pursuing a fit body, or snobby for wanting to learn new things. You'll have to be comfortable with that or, even better, not give a shit. With great wealth, you have the opportunity to help many more people than if you were stuck in the middle class. Money doesn't corrupt people or make them evil. It's simply an amplifier. It turns up the volume on the kind of person you already are. If you're a jerk, you'll just be a louder jerk with money. If you're a generous person, you can be even more generous with a lot of money. Physical fitness isn't an indicator of vanity—it's a desire to live in a well-functioning "machine" that isn't always breaking down. Pursuing knowledge doesn't make you snobby—it means you realize the more you learn, the more you don't know. The world is vast and full of incredible experiences and opportunities. Don't limit yourself to what's on Netflix this month.

Motivation comes in two forms: prize and pain, carrot and stick. Being motivated by pain can be incredibly helpful, but if your life isn't painful enough, it's your job to figure out the prize you want to strive for.

What's the Point?

Being motivated by pain or prize is great, but something I've said for a while now is that motivation is a fickle mistress. It's a handy tool to have in your toolbox when you get started or when you need it, but motivation will ultimately fail you in the long run. That's where having a purpose comes in. Having a *why* is incredibly important. And you might be asking, "Chris, isn't my *why* just another form of motivation?" I think there's a difference. Your *why* should run deeper, and it isn't affected by emotions. It is an ideal to strive for.

The *why* can be vastly different for different people. Some may want to become successful because people in their lives told them they couldn't do it. Some may want to use their status to help their family or find a mate. Some may want to change the system (and the only way to do that is by becoming successful within the system). I say all of this to point out that your *why* will likely be very different from someone else's. Get used to saying, who cares? Don't feel obligated to have a "noble" *why*. As long as it's important enough to you to provoke long-lasting change, it doesn't matter what it is. What I'm saying is that your *why* is one of the most important things you will discover on this journey. It has to be significant enough to invoke action, regardless of your feelings.

Starting out, you may not quite know what your *why* is, and that's fine at the beginning. But to ensure long-lasting sustainability on this journey, you need to figure it out. Think about what will drive you toward the life you want after your motivation has dwindled and all you're left with is the work that needs to be done. If you've racked your brain and still don't know what your *why* is, start anyway and figure it out later.

"Okay, Chris, but *how* do I figure out what my *why* is?" That's an excellent question. If you've spent serious time trying to figure it out and have still come up with nothing, try attacking it from another angle. Ask yourself what you *don't* want your purpose to be.

So, what is *my* purpose? What is *my why*? I can confidently say that one purpose of mine is to be the epitome of human excellence. I want to be an absolute monster in every area of my life. Mentally, I want to be sharp and well-read. Financially, I want to have the freedom to do anything I want, wherever I want, whenever I want, and however I want. Emotionally, I want my presence to be felt when I walk into a room, and not because I inspire chaos, but rather because I'm overwhelmingly calm. My *why* is the desire to embody excellence because anything less than that is a disservice to the opportunity I have in living. Excellence is the goal. Excellence in all things.

"But Chris, that doesn't make *me* happy. That isn't fulfilling *my* truth." My response? Just shut up. Your first truth should be bettering yourself, aiming for excellence in all areas, and living in a way that provides value to those around you. "But, Chris, I feel strongly about the stray cat population in my area." I don't care, and neither does anybody else. But if that's your *why*, other people's feelings or thoughts shouldn't stop you. My point is that you should pursue excellence to help whatever cause *you* deem important.

I get super irritated when people who clearly don't care about themselves ask for a handout to help a cause that hardly matters to anybody. If you don't have your act together, I don't care about the cause you're passionate about because it says to me that you're just trying to derive importance and significance from something outside yourself so you don't feel so miserable. Try this instead: become excellent in all areas of your life. Get in shape, clean yourself up, and be able to speak intelligently to others. Get your emotions in check. Express passion intelligently. When you come at me as someone who cares about yourself, I'm more likely to hear what you're passionate about and what concerns you.

I've always found it difficult to come up with a personal mission statement or a personal vision for my life. How do I sum up the reason for my existence using only a few words? However, if I'm unable to concisely communicate what I do and am supposed to do, how much of a grasp do I have on my own personal purpose? Something I've found that helps is knowing what my purpose is *not*. Then, through a slow, drawn-out process of elimination, I can narrow down what I think my purpose might be.

So again, what is my purpose? My purpose is to become the embodiment of human excellence and to help others do that as well. And I feel pretty good about that. Early concepts of this book kind of revolved around the idea of achieving the ninetieth percentile of human existence or being in the top 10 percent in all areas of life. A question that then comes up is, why bother trying to be in the top 10 percent? If you have to ask that question, this book might not be for you. But for the sake of being thorough, I'll try to answer. The short answer is that you should try because it's possible, and you can probably achieve it. Think of how much better the world would be—and how much better off the people in it would be—if more people achieved their potential. What would happen if more people pursued excellent health, both mentally and physically? What would happen if people tried really hard to become wealthier? And not because they necessarily needed to but because they could.

I was thinking about the phrase "a rising tide raises all ships." What if we aren't the ships? What if you view the ships as outliers—people who need help—and the tide as the general public? If you raise the standard of the general public, the tide, and everybody is achieving their internal potential and living as healthy and wealthy as they possibly can, then the few who are actually struggling, need help, and require some assistance and maybe some support navigating life's storms will be lifted by the tide, and their standard of living will improve. The rising tide of healthy, wealthy, caring, and mentally resilient people can lift the ships of those who are struggling and can use just a little bit of support to get through a particular storm.

So, maybe the goal is just to do better in the world. And if that's the case, you need to be the best version of yourself to do it. Even if that isn't your goal, I still think the act of pursuing excellence will affect those around you in a positive way, whether you meant for it to happen or not. A better world will come about from your pursuit of excellence than if you choose to stay comfortable and stagnant.

Exercise: Life Purpose

This next little bit is a quick exercise. I want you to begin to define your purpose. If you know exactly what you're supposed to be doing in your life, I want you to write it down, circle it, underline it, and highlight it. If you're not quite sure yet what your true purpose is, begin by listing all the things you *don't* want your life to mean. If you write down all the things you don't want your purpose to be, then through a process of elimination and examination of those things, you'll begin to better understand what your true purpose is.

Life Purpose (What is my *why?*)

_____

_____

_____

_____

_____

_____

_____

From Zero to Hero

Here's the bottom line. The greatest return on investment comes from investing in yourself.

But how do you go about investing in yourself? And where do you start? The fastest way to move from mediocrity to excellence is consistency. If you are an average Joe or an average Jane, being consistent is the best way to achieve excellence and high-end performance in all areas of life. Begin where you are, find the habits that are working well, and continue doing them. However, if you are an absolute dirtbag who has nothing at all going for you, the fastest way to move up to average Joe status is just starting. Once you've begun and have started making progress toward average, apply consistency and drive on. The point behind this is that if you are at rock bottom and can barely get your act together enough to take a shower every day, you just need to *get started*. Start caring about hygiene—brush your teeth, shower, and put on clean clothes.

Starting is an often-dismissed step in this whole process, but it's arguably the most important. This reminds me of David Goggins. If you're not familiar with his story, check out the video where he describes his upbringing and, ultimately, his physical and mental state before becoming the baddest dude on the planet.[2] He hit rock bottom before he started making drastic changes in his life to become excellent.

Scan the QR code for David's story:

So, if you're at a point in life where you have nowhere else to go but up, the fastest way to move in that direction is to take that first step—whatever that step may look like—and just start. And if you're that average guy or gal who aspires to excellence and wants to reach the top tier of human performance, then it's important not only to start but to maintain consistency.

So, going back to my earlier question, what is your truth? Well, no one cares until you've expressed that you give a shit about yourself. Now, before a bunch of you get your panties in a wad, let me explain. There's a big difference between investing in yourself to make your life and the lives of those around you better and becoming an energy and resource "vampire" who sucks the life out of those around you to elevate yourself. People often think that life is a zero-sum game. If I'm winning, that means somebody else is losing. But I don't think life has to be that way. You can totally crush life and also actively

---

[2] Goggins, D. A., *Can't Hurt Me: Master Your Mind and Defy the Odds.* https://openlibrary.org/books/OL28024418M/Can't_Hurt_Me.

help those around you win. Life can be a win-win. My recommendation is for you to win and help others win, too.

The Ouroboros

When I got out of the military back in 2022, I started a personal development and mindset coaching business called Ouroboros Solutions, LLC. The Ouroboros is an ancient symbol of a snake eating its own tail. As the snake devours the pieces of itself that are no longer necessary, no longer serving it, no longer providing value, it gets the strength to grow and become better. That's what I see when I look at the Ouroboros, and that's what inspired me to name my company after it. Often, when people are deciding to make a change in their life, they're actually looking for something to add to their life. Maybe it's the latest new workout routine or the new fad diet, or maybe it's the new gadget that's going to streamline their life and make everything better. That's one approach, but I think what would serve most people best is just doing a life audit and asking what they can start *eliminating* from their lives. What can I remove because it's no longer serving me and no longer providing me with benefits or value? What would my life look like if I took that away?

Another thing to keep in mind throughout this process is guarding against time and energy "vampires." We all intuitively know what these are, but to make things abundantly clear, I'll spell it out. A time and energy "vampire" is anything in our lives that takes away our time and energy with little to no actual return on that investment.

My favorite philosopher, Ayn Rand, differentiates between investment and sacrifice. She describes a sacrifice as the trading of something of high value for something of lesser value. And that's exactly what "vampires" do. They entice you to sacrifice your most precious commodity, which is time, for something that provides little to no return for that trade. Some easy examples are mindlessly scrolling on social media, constantly seeking out that next dopamine hit, or binge-watching for hours on Netflix or Hulu. Another example that might be a little bit more difficult to wrap your mind around is people. There are people out there who drain you of your time and energy. As you read that line, I'm sure at least one or two people came to mind. So again, we intuitively know how to spot these "vampires." They are nasty little things, and when they're people, it can be difficult to navigate the situation. Later on in the book, I'll describe how to deal with people who are "vampires" in your life. Sometimes it's as simple as spending less time with them so they stop sucking the energy out of your life.

So, what does the elimination process look like? It needs to begin with an honest evaluation. Sit down and ask yourself, "Does this benefit me and drive me toward my desired end state?" If the answer is yes, right on, keep it. If the answer is no, start to explore what your life would look like if you eliminated or reduced its presence in your life. What would your health and mental clarity be like if you had only two beers instead of six? What would it look like if you went clubbing only one night a week instead of two? How would it affect your bank account? What would your energy levels look like if you stopped hanging out with people who don't respect you and your time? What would your waistline look like if you cut 250 calories out of your diet every day? How would your sleep schedule change for the better if you stopped crushing Red Bulls all afternoon? I think this process of elimination is necessary for anyone pursuing excellence. The concept of the Ouroboros—seeking out the things that you can actively eliminate—is a great way to make improvements in your life. It's not necessarily finding that perfect fad diet or that new workout gadget on Amazon. Rather, it's asking what time I am going to bed, how much TV I am watching, and how much TikTok I am scrolling. What if it was fifteen minutes instead of an hour of TikTok a day?

Sometimes, it's just being honest with yourself and questioning how much time you're spending on things that don't provide you with much value. What would your life look like if you began to eliminate those things? And if you can't completely get rid of those things, what if you just aimed at reducing their presence in your life?

Exercise: Time and Energy "Vampires"

In the space provided, list several things you can begin to eliminate. If you're having trouble coming up with things, ask yourself if there are any time and energy "vampires" in the following areas: excessive time on social media or Netflix, unnecessary spending, negative people or relationships, junk food, and so on.

Mental:

_____

_____

_____

Emotional:

_____

_____

_____

Physical:

_____

_____

_____

Social:

_____

_____

_____

Financial:

_____

_____

_____

Your Most Precious Commodity

Time is your most precious commodity. There's a well-known analogy comparing time to an imaginary bank account. Every day, we're given a deposit of 86,400 seconds, and we get to use that deposit however we want. So it's like getting a little over $86,000, but it never rolls over—once the day's up, you don't get to keep any that's left over. The goal is to invest it and use it as wisely as you can to better your tomorrow and set you up for future success. Full disclosure: When I hear things like this, I often give a quick nod of acknowledgment because there's truth behind it. We are incredibly fortunate that we wake up each day to that deposit of 86,400 seconds.

I acknowledge it's true, but I often kind of shrug it off and go about my day because it didn't have the impact that the original author intended. But I'd like to tell you about a realization I came to years ago while I was listening to a podcast. I remember I was doing yard work at a friend's house, and as I listened to the podcast, the speaker made a very interesting point. In America, on average, we live approximately 4,000 weeks. That's only 28,000 days. I remember stopping in my tracks as I was raking leaves. It was at that moment that I no longer looked at life as this perpetual bank account with endless deposits. Rather, I started to look at it as a countdown. And maybe this is a little dark, but I tell you, it really changed my perspective on how I wanted to live.

I journaled a lot during that time in my life, and I remember I started including a countdown next to the date of each new entry. I was in my early to mid-twenties at that point, and I remember doing the calculations. *If I'm in my twenties, how many weeks have I lived already? And if that's the case, how many days do I have left if the average individual lives 28,000 days?* I remember tallying it up, and the number was a lot smaller than I had hoped. In order to create a reminder to maintain this sense of urgency in my life, when I would journal, I would put the date for that particular entry, but I would also include the countdown. I stopped taking days for granted, and truthfully, listening to that podcast and embracing the concept that our days are limited was the beginning of my pursuit of a different future.

There's an old saying that I'll paraphrase here: The best time to plant a tree was ten years ago, and the second best time is today. Sometimes I talk with clients, and they get frustrated because they're coming to the realization that we should really be capitalizing on the opportunities that life provides on a daily basis. They're frustrated because they're no longer in their twenties, and they think, *Man, I wish I could go back and begin implementing all these routines in my life to achieve all the goals I wanted earlier in life.*

And I totally get it. There's a little bit of heartache when you come to this realization. I just turned forty, and that was a bit of a wake-up call for me, too, but when you're hitting forty, and you're looking back, you're like, *Man, if I was eighteen, this is the advice I would give myself.* Yes, of course, it would be better if you had started a long time ago, but don't get so wrapped around the axle about having not started sooner that you don't start now. Don't regret missed opportunities longer than you need to. If you didn't start ten years ago, start today. That's kind of what I'm trying to say here. Focus on the opportunity that you have right now—today—and then invest heavily into it and ensure that tomorrow, and the next day, and the next day are improving gradually. As I mentioned before, it's my opinion that time is your most precious commodity. Once a minute is gone, you can never get it back.

Exercise: 4000 Weeks

Take a few minutes and calculate how many weeks you have left in your life. If the average American lives for approximately 4000 weeks, how many weeks do you have left? Here's how to find the answer. Take your current age and multiply it by 52 (the number of weeks in a year). Whatever number you come up with, subtract that from 4000. If you're thirty-seven years old, you've lived 1,924 weeks. Subtract that from 4000, and you're left with 2,076. This exercise isn't meant to depress you but rather create a sense of urgency to pursue excellence every day.

_____ (current age) x 52 (weeks in a year) = _____ (current age in weeks) 4,000 (weeks average American lives) − _____ (age in weeks) = _____ (weeks left)

A helpful practice I have a lot of my clients do is to conduct audits on various areas of life. For example: if somebody comes to me and says they desperately want to lose a lot of weight, I'm like, cool. Don't change anything about your diet yet, but document everything you eat and the calories and macros associated with that food. Do that for two weeks. The reason I encourage this is that if you know what your baseline is—if you know that for two weeks on average, you consume this many calories, this much protein, this much fat, and this many carbs on a daily basis—you know exactly what you do from day to day. Now, you're able to adjust it to a caloric deficit to lose weight or a caloric surplus if you're trying to put on weight.

Doing the above gives you data on yourself, and once you have that, you can adjust your behavior. It's the same with a time audit in that you look at your day and what you did each hour. Of course, some of those hours are going to be spent sleeping and some eating food or traveling to work, and that's fine. But you'll start to notice patterns. Even though you didn't think you were, you were actually spending a lot of time watching TV or scrolling through social media. And if you can be honest with yourself and take note of all of the time spent in various areas of your life, you can objectively look at your life and realize that you weren't quite where you thought you were and needed to make some adjustments. Similarly, you can do a sleep audit and note not only the hours you've slept but also the times that you went to bed and got up and the quality of your sleep. Maybe you start to notice a pattern that if you get six hours of sleep, you're on the struggle bus the next day, and if you get eight and a half hours, you still wake up feeling kind of groggy. But if you get seven and a half hours of sleep, that's the sweet spot. And that's what you should strive to get every day, to be better the next day.

Something I often tell my clients is that wherever you are in life, it is almost 100 percent a result of the decisions you've made, the habits you've developed, and the actions you've taken up until this point. In other words, if you're unsatisfied with where you are in life, you have only to look in the mirror to see who is responsible and no one is coming to rescue you. This may rub some people the wrong way, and that's okay. Expecting others to fix your future is the wrong approach. Expecting others to bail you out is a huge mistake. We'll dig into this concept a little deeper in the next chapter.

Becoming too dependent on your government, your parents or your spouse just makes you a more dependent individual in the long run. And I want to qualify this by saying that there are definitely times in life when you need help, and you should have a circle of people around you that you can reach out to for support. Expecting others to constantly bail you out is a huge mistake, but surrounding yourself with high-quality people is absolutely vital—so vital that it has its own chapter that you'll have the opportunity to check out later.

I want to reiterate that where you end up in life is entirely up to you. I think the biggest enemy of improvement and growth is complacency. Having your needs adequately met and not being bored is the fastest and most permanent way to mediocrity. Breaking free from comfort is harder than breaking free from misery. When you're not satisfied, when you're at rock bottom or in some kind of pain, the decision to change and the discipline to move toward a goal is easy. When you're comfortable, though, there's significantly less drive to push forward and improve. It gets even worse when you've allowed yourself to be comfortable for years or decades.

The scary truth about the acceptance of comfort is that it allows you to slowly lower your standards in all areas of life. Kind of like an insidious cancer, it slowly eats away at one's resolve, and the end result is the acceptance of a lifestyle, physique, bank balance, and mental acuity equivalent to that of a total slob. So, what's the solution? Begin to feel uncomfortable when things get too comfortable. This might sound a little backward, but I've begun to crave the feeling of being on this precipice that separates me from success and failure. I kind of want to be right on that edge because I want to push to the edge of my own abilities. If success is guaranteed, it isn't really a challenge, and so you can still kind of hide in that comfort zone. I encourage you to enjoy the uncertainty of the outcome.

I'm not a fan of participation trophies, and I preach against them constantly. That was actually a big motivator for me to join the Army because I wanted to pursue something where success was not guaranteed. I wanted to be able to give everything I had toward a particular goal, like becoming a Green Beret or starting a business. I wanted to be able to put everything I had toward it, even if I still might come up short. The risk of failure is part of the reason that those journeys enticed me.

I've been met with a whole list of why people's lives are miserable, various reasons and excuses as to why they're unfulfilled, but very rarely do people point the finger at themselves. And please don't think I'm some callous jerk who doesn't take into account circumstances totally outside of your control, like tragic accidents or diseases. I'm not saying that it's your fault that those things happened to you. Some of us just get dealt a horrible hand in life, and I don't want to diminish that. But what I'm saying is that your response to the hand you're dealt is entirely your responsibility.

Exercise: Rocking Chair Test

I'm going to wrap up this chapter by giving you the "Rocking Chair test." As you're reading these lines, I want you to picture yourself toward the end of your life. Maybe you're eighty or ninety years old, sitting on your rocking chair, and enjoying a cool spring breeze that's blowing across your porch as you look out over your property. I want you to look back on your life and ask yourself if you're happy with how your life turned out. As you're sitting there rocking in your chair, are you filled with regret for all the missed opportunities in your life that you didn't chase after? Are you totally content knowing that the doors that closed on certain opportunities set you up for success in pursuing new opportunities? Are you excited about where you ended up? Or are you riddled with regret because you were a little too nervous and apprehensive to go after opportunities that may have been a little bit scary? Are you happy, content, and fulfilled with the direction your life took? Are the relationships in your life meaningful? Are you surrounded by people who love you and care about you?

_____

_____

_____

_____

_____

Recommended Reading

Atlas Shrugged by Ayn Rand

The 12-Week Year by Brian Moran and Michael Lennington

CHAPTER 2

Who the Hell Are You?

"What Am I doing with my soul? Interrogate yourself to find out what inhabits your so-called mind and what kind of soul you have now. A child's soul, an adolescent's, a woman's? A tyrant's soul? The soul of a predator—or its prey?"

–Marcus Aurelius[3]

A Bit of My Journey

I want to begin this chapter with a little bit of a story. It's going to be a story that kind of leads up to my enlistment into the United States Army but also relates to a very pivotal situation I had to deal with when I was on my last team. I joined the Army a little bit later in life. I was twenty-eight years old, and I remember the moment that I knew I needed to do something. I was working at a fancy hotel in Virginia. The dining room was a little short-staffed, so they asked me and a couple of other people to help out with handing out food to the patrons at the restaurant. I was like, "Yeah, sure, no problem." I was holding a tray of drinks or food over my head, and I was walking to the table, and it was right then that I thought, *I want to do more with my life.* Working there was great. I loved the people, and it was an excellent opportunity. But I was getting comfortable. You know, my bills were

---

[3] Aurelius, M., *Meditations: A New Translation* (Modern Library, 2003), 58.

getting paid, and it was a relatively safe job. But I wanted more. I was getting too content. I was getting too comfortable. And interestingly, that made me very uncomfortable.

I knew I needed to do something different. So then, I was like, *I'm going to join the Army.* I talked to several recruiters and eventually found one. He and I got to working together and started working out pretty heavily. And throughout that process, that initial contact, I did a lot of research. I asked myself, *What kind of job do I want in the Army?* I knew I wanted to really push myself, so I decided I wanted to be Special Forces. I wanted to be a Green Beret. After talking with my recruiter about it—and that research process took about six months to a year—I thought it aligned with the kind of interest I had and the direction I wanted to take my life. My recruiter thought I'd be a good candidate.

We have what's called an "18X contract," which essentially means you enlist, and the contract guarantees that as long as you pass basic training and survive airborne school, you get a shot at trying out for Special Forces. I was like, *Yeah, that's the one I want.* Fast forward, I was training one day, climbing a mountain with a buddy of mine, and my knee started to hurt pretty bad, which resulted in me having to go to the doctor. I told him my knee hurt, and I was trying to join the Army. He said, "Well, that's the knee you had surgery on when you were a kid. There's probably very little cartilage in there, so I don't think the military's in the cards for you." I was devastated.

Having worked out forever and gotten through this process, working with a recruiter and stuff, I knew what I wanted to do in life. And then this doctor tells me that because of a previous knee injury, it was probably not going to happen. So, I was super bummed and had a poopy face, but I kept working out, but kind of half-hearted. And then I decided I was going to sign up for one of those mud races. If I did well at it, then maybe I'd go see another doctor and give it a second shot.

I remember it was a Rugged Maniac in Richmond, Virginia. I'd been training for quite a while, and I totally won my heat and then scored pretty high within the rankings. You know, I didn't win the thing, but I was pretty pleased with myself—and that was my sign. I went and talked to a different doctor and told him my situation. I wanted to join the Army, and I wanted to be a Green Beret. My knee was giving me some issues, but I was still performing relatively well. He grabbed my knee, kind of manipulated it a little bit, and said, "Yeah, I think you're probably pretty good. If you're able to do the training, go for it, man."

After that, I talked to the recruiter. He said he was taking me to the facility where I'd do my physical and get sworn in, and I'd be good to go. So, we get there, and it's a whole day's process. They gave me a bunch of tests and made me squat and duck-walk around to be sure I was physically capable of serving in the military. And everything went totally fine. At the end of the day, there was an exit interview with the head physician. When I went to his office, he told me to have a seat and then asked me what I wanted to do in the Army. I told him I wanted to try out for Special Forces because I think it really aligned with my interests and what I wanted to push myself toward. He said, "That's great. Those guys are awesome. I've worked with them."

He was looking through my medical file, and he got to a point where he said he wanted to check something really quickly. He walked over to his shelf, pulled a big military medical book down, opened it up, and flipped through a couple of pages. Then he said, "Oh man, I'm sorry, son, but because you had this knee surgery when you were younger, it prevents you from signing any kind of airborne contract from here." When I asked him what that meant, he told me he couldn't give me a Special Forces 18X contract there. I was just devastated. He told me I could still enlist in the Army, but I just couldn't get an airborne contract. When I talked to my recruiter and told him what the doc had just told me, he said I could enlist as an 11B or an infantryman, and then hopefully, maybe during basic training, I could pick up a Special Forces contract once there. At this point, I was already mentally and emotionally committed to this process. So I said, "Let's do it."

And so, I enlisted as 11B, and then a couple of weeks into basic training, some Special Forces recruiters approached me and several other guys in the platoon and asked if we'd try out. I signed my name on the dotted line, and that moved me through the rest of basic training. I got through Airborne School with no injuries, made it through selection, and then three years of the Q Course. The Q Course was miserable and super long. It was just a marathon of trying to show up every day and be excellent.

But I want to get to this part. I graduated from the Q Course and earned my Green Beret during a time when they were doing "freefalls for all." Well, "freefalls for all" is referencing Military Freefall School or High Altitude, Low Opening (HALO) School. It's a cool-guy school that everybody wants to go to, and they were just giving it to everybody who graduated, and everybody was stoked.

So, I went to freefall school in Yuma, Arizona, and learned how to exit aircraft from high altitudes. In regular airborne school, your parachute is actually connected to the aircraft. And so, as you jump out, it deploys the parachute for you, and then you land like a sack of potatoes. It's not a very soft landing. But in HALO, or freefall school, it's more similar to skydiving. You pull your own ripcord, you have an altimeter, you're in charge of steering your parachute, and if done correctly, you can actually land pretty softly on your feet.

I graduated and then immediately got orders to Stuttgart, Germany, at Panzer Kaserne. That was where my first team was, and they were all super salty because some brand-new guy got freefall school right out of the pipeline. And for the three years I was there, I actually didn't jump freefall very often. Not only did the weather in Germany not always cooperate when we tried to do airborne operations, but again, my team was super salty and didn't like the fact that some new guy got freefall.

Then, I got orders to move back to Fort Carson, Colorado, in the States. Every Special Forces team has different kinds of specialties. There are dive teams that do a lot of water stuff, mobility guys that operate various kinds of vehicles, ruck teams that just throw everything in a backpack and walk wherever they're going—and then there are freefall teams. I was very excited to be assigned to this team. My teammates were very senior, very well-versed, and very experienced. Three of them had actually been instructors at the freefall school, and they had thousands and thousands of jumps between them. Interestingly, my first trip with this team was back to Arizona to do a requalification, which is really just making sure everybody's skills are up to par to ensure that they can be safe in the sky, navigate their parachutes with one another, and land in a specific place.

So, we went to Arizona, and again, I was kind of the brand-new guy on the team. I'd been in a group for a number of years, but I was new to this team, so I was still trying to figure out my pecking order. I remembered we were doing a Hollywood jump, or a slick jump—which is just your parachute, your helmet, and altimeter—on a Monday morning. And I was pretty nervous because, again, it had been a while since I'd done freefall.

We got out to the aircraft and loaded up, and I was kind of in the middle of the stack because the senior guys were up front, and the very senior guys were in the back to navigate this chaos. When the aircraft got up to 12,000 to 14,000 feet, the ramp at the back dropped open, so now you had all this air rushing by. And again, I was nervous because I hadn't done this in a while. We got the green light to exit the plane. The first couple of guys moved to the edge of the ramp and dove out. And I was like, all right, let's do this. I dove out, and I got on heading. I checked my altimeter, I pulled my ripcord, and everything went perfectly, just like riding a bike. I remembered how to do the whole process. When I landed, I thought, *Okay, I've got this!* As the week progressed, we started to add more and more equipment leading up to Friday, when we were doing what's called a "wall locker jump," where everything in our wall locker would be attached to us.

So I had a big rucksack between my legs, and my rifle was strapped across my waist. I had an oxygen tank, a hose, and a mask. I had a chest ring that had GPS on it, a big compass, and obviously, my helmet and radio and stuff like that. We were pretty weighed down at this point as we waddled out to the aircraft. Because I'd had no issues throughout the whole week, I was feeling pretty good about this jump. We entered the aircraft, loaded up, and got up to an altitude between 12,000 and 14,000 feet. The ramp dropped open, and the first couple of guys exited. I got to the edge of the ramp, dove out, and got on heading. I checked my altimeter, pulled my ripcord, and looked up, only to discover I had line twists, which meant the lines going from the harness to the parachute had become twisted. It wasn't a huge deal, and it's usually a pretty quick fix—you just grab them, pull them apart, kind of untwist them, and you're good to go. But as I was doing that, the parachute kicked me out sideways, so I was parallel to the earth, and then I began to spiral.

The reason all of this happened is because freefall parachutes are designed a little bit differently than regular airborne parachutes. Freefall parachutes are very much like a wing, and as they fall, they create forward drive so you can actually glide or fly to your destination, even over long distances. Well, as I was untwisting myself, my chute kicked me out sideways, driving me toward the ground simply because of the way the parachute is designed.

As I began to spiral, I was getting kind of nervous. Somebody more intelligent or more senior on the team would have just cut that parachute away and deployed their reserve, and they would have been totally fine. But I was super stubborn or dumb or both and was just riding that wave. As I was whipping through the sky, I was losing altitude, and my vision was beginning to close in. Finally, at the last second, before I blacked out, I managed to untwist my lines. I grabbed my brakes and yanked them, and it leveled me out. I was now flying a good canopy, and I wasn't plummeting toward the earth anymore. But now I was incredibly dizzy, very nauseous, and totally disoriented.

I was looking all around the sky and couldn't find anybody. I didn't know where anyone else was. And that's when they all started yelling over the radio. "Chris, turn around, you're going the wrong way!" "Chris, go left. No, your *other* left!" "Chris, check your GPS!" I looked down at my chest rig and saw that the GPS was spinning in circles because my equilibrium was all jacked up. And that's when we got a break in the radio chatter. Matt, a super senior guy on the team, came over the radio. He said, "Chris, turn toward the sun."

We'd been jumping in the morning, and our drop zone was generally east of us. The sun was directly behind me, so I hit a hard left turn and started flying toward the sun. At about that time, my buddy Andy swooped in front of me and was able to guide me to the drop zone. We all landed together.

Later that evening, I took Matt out for a beer or two because I definitely owed him. "Chris," he said, "what you experienced today is what I call the 'phoenix phenomenon.' And I call it that because, you know, in all of our parachutes, we have a device called a 'Cypress.' If you were to exit the aircraft while unconscious and you were falling at terminal velocity, once you hit a certain altitude, the 'Cypress' would recognize that something was wrong and fire and deploy your reserve parachute for you so you could land relatively safely. Because you were spiraling, you weren't falling fast enough for that to engage. You would have just burned into the ground like a phoenix."

So, what's the point of this story? The "phoenix phenomenon" that I experienced in the military sort of became the core principle behind my coaching philosophy. In my story, because I was nauseous and disoriented from dizziness, I relied on the fixed sun in the sky to help me adjust my course. We need that in life, too. We need something off in the distance that we can reference as we're overwhelmed with day-to-day stuff, something we can look at and say, "All right, I'm still on track. I'm still on course to where I want to be. I'm just dealing with a little bit of craziness right now." Conversely, you might look up and realize you're way off course, and then you can adjust accordingly to get back on track and move forward.

This whole chapter is about figuring out who you want to be because I think that is the most important test. It's that sun in the sky that I'm trying to help you establish. Knowing who you want to be is the most important question you can ask yourself. So, that's the takeaway.

A Reality Check

The following is an excerpt from the workbook I use with all of my clients. Ask yourself if any of this sounds familiar.

"Stagnation has a cumulative effect. The cost of staying where you are is putting on extra weight, which makes you not want to train, which means you gain more weight. Before you know it, you're thirty pounds heavier than a healthy you should be. You stop reading books because Netflix is easier and doesn't require anything from you, and you slowly become boring. You have nothing interesting to talk about because you've filled your brain with the latest episode of *The Kardashians* or *The Walking Dead*. You've chosen to not learn a new skill or master an interesting subject, and so you're just like everyone else. You're anxious all the time and have trouble focusing on anything longer than three minutes because TikTok has conditioned you to have the attention span of a goldfish. This will lead to being forgetful and scatterbrained. At first, you chalk it up to getting older, but in actuality, you've simply chosen not to train your mind by practicing meditation. Your relationship with your kids suffers because you're too tired to play with them or too addicted to your phone to listen to them, and your spouse is growing more frustrated with you because the passion has left the relationship. They feel like they are getting your leftovers because you haven't been intentional with the time you spend with them. They've become an afterthought instead of a priority. Then you are confused when you come home one day, and they're not there. You're barely making ends meet. Bills always seem due, and you can't even remember your last ten purchases, but you can tell me exactly how your Fantasy Football team is doing and who's winning the league so far. The cost of doing nothing is slow and insidious. It sneaks up on you, and before you know it, you're nowhere near where you wanted to be at this stage of your life."

If you aren't completely satisfied with who you are as a person, decide right now who you would like to be. From this point on, act like the person you want to become. Healthy people exercise, smart people learn new things, rich people manage their money and invest, and loyal people spend time with and invest in others. That may not sound like much of an answer, but throughout this book, you'll learn that there isn't a quick fix to any of the problems mentioned. It requires behavioral changes, and the effects you're seeking will take time.

A Virtual Reality Check

There's an interesting theory that everything around us is just a big simulation. And if that's the case, none of this really matters because it's all part of a game. I don't necessarily believe this theory, but I think it creates an interesting thought experiment.

If this is all just a giant video game we're playing, that means the difficult tasks are ways to level up and improve one's ability to perform in the game. If life is just a big simulation, what kind of character do you want to become? How would you level up your character in the game? Start living that way.

Pretend you're playing this third-person shooter, and you get to observe all the things that are happening to your avatar. They aren't actually happening to you, but you're able to react and think through various scenarios in a very detached manner because you're observing things that are happening to your character. If you've ever read *The Untethered Soul* or *The Surrender Experiment* by Michael Singer, this will sound kind of familiar. The ability to detach from your character's circumstances allows you to think clearly and make the best decisions to allow you to advance through the game.

Additionally, you have the freedom to make decisions without emotion and focus on what's best for your character. If we approached life as though we were living in a simulation or a game, it would allow us the freedom to make decisions detached from emotion and focused entirely on whether a particular path was what was best for our character's survival or advancement.

Pretend you're a third-person shooter watching things unfold. Every skill you learn levels up your avatar. Every dollar you earn enables you to buy more resources, tools, or weapons to better equip you for the adventure. An interesting thing about this concept is it allows you to explore different personalities or personas to navigate life. In this scenario, you are the safe observer. Nothing can touch you. The avatar may be affected, but you, as the observer, are safe on the other side of the screen. Maybe this is a silly thought experiment, but maybe it's the permission you need to act how you want.

Do you want to be a hero? Act the way a hero does. Do you want to be a villain? What's stopping you? Do you want to get rich? Well, then, play the game. Do you want to get super yoked or buff? Level up in the gym. Do you want to end a toxic relationship? Detach and make the decision from the safe side of your computer screen. Every decision either progresses you further in the game or moves you backward.

Additionally, if this is just a game, failures don't mean anything. What others think of you doesn't really mean anything. Things that tend to paralyze a normal person no longer apply to the person who is detached. And even if we aren't in a simulation, pretending that you are gives you something others don't have: the freedom to pursue your own adventure.

My friend often gets discouraged because he doesn't know what he wants to do with his life. He struggles with finding purpose. Imagine if he realized he could create his own meaning in life. He gets to become significant (in his own eyes) because he's playing the game. Just like in a video game, leveling up requires a degree of dedication and some vision as to who you want to become. I would recommend thinking about all the attributes you would want your character to have and then identifying the *what* that is required to level up to that ideal in your own life. Get very clear about the values you want to have, and establish specific non-negotiable standards you're going to live by. I think a system of ethics should be established long before it's ever required in a specific situation. Ethics help us when we engage with others, but I think they also help with how we engage with ourselves.

Self-Respect Is a Non-negotiable

Respect from others begins with respect for self. Don't tolerate behavior from yourself that you wouldn't want from someone else. Negative self-talk has to go. Engaging in habits that destroy you needs to stop. Start talking to yourself as if you were a really good friend you cared about and wanted the best for. I've found this process of self-love often begins with forgiveness. Past failures are something we all have to deal with. Some of us have bigger failures than others, but regardless of the decisions you may have made in the past, moving forward will be difficult if you don't forgive yourself first.

Exercise: Forgiveness

Buckle up—this one will be uncomfortable. It has to be done, though, before we get to the next exercise. Take just a couple of minutes to write down three things you have not forgiven yourself for. Once you've written them down, I want you to go into your bathroom, look at yourself in the mirror, and tell yourself that you forgive yourself and love yourself. I think this is an important part of the process because often when we're trying to pursue a particular identity—the kind of person we want to be—we get hung up on past failures and mistakes that hinder our ability to dream big. Forgiveness is not forgetting mistakes or failures you may have made but rather acknowledging that they existed. Forgiveness is looking at yourself in the mirror and truly wanting what is best for you as you move forward.

_____

_____

_____

_____

_____

We all ascribe to some kind of identity. Our identity is an accumulation of previous decisions, actions, and habits. More often than not, we allow our daily habits and actions to decide for us what that identity is. In other words, our working identity is mostly reactionary, not intentional. I think we need to recalibrate this process. We need to first decide who we want to become and then make decisions, perform actions, and develop habits in accordance with that desired identity. I hate it when people say things like, "I'm just too lazy to do that," or "My brain just doesn't work that way," or "I'd never be able to do that." I hate it because their words make it true. These statements are identities people ascribe to based on decisions, actions, and habits *up until now*. If, however, they were to plan backward and dictate the direction of their life rather than merely react to it, they could identify with statements like "I'm the most productive person I know," or "I used to struggle to understand this, but now it comes super easy to me," or "Believe it or not, I wasn't always good at this. It took me a while to master."

Everything begins with an identity. Who are you? That's an easy question to answer. Your identity is not what you *want* to be. It's the accumulation of your daily actions. You may say you're a super successful entrepreneur, a world-class athlete, or a Buddhist monk on the brink of enlightenment, but do your daily actions support these claims? Look at what you do every day because if your daily actions consist of scrolling through social media, binge-watching the latest Netflix shows, or consuming piles of junk food, then, in actuality, *that* is your identity. You have allowed life to happen to you, and you are merely reacting to it. As a result of your actions, you've lost all of your passion or fuel to pursue excellence. We all know being addicted to your phone is unhealthy. We all know inhaling junk food is killing you. And we all know numbing your mind with television makes you dumb. But you don't have any more energy to put out because you're reacting all day and have been for years.

So how do you fix this? Change your identity! Decide who you want to be, and then let that decision drive your daily actions. If you want to be CEO of a major company, do CEO-type things every day. If you want to be Mr. Olympia in five years, start doing things Mr. Olympia would do—find a trainer and follow a strict program and diet. The point is that you can know exactly who you are right now by looking at your daily actions. And if you want to be something greater, that future version of yourself needs to drive your habits in the present. But the best part is that you get to decide. So, I ask again, who are you? If you were to change nothing and continue down the path that you're on, would you be satisfied with the person you're becoming? Better yet, are you excited about that person? Are you stoked about the person you're evolving into? If the answer is anything less than a strong yes, then something needs to change. That change begins with deciding who you want to become. Once that decision is made, the rest of the process will be easy.

Maybe you feel like you can't focus or like you're never quite making ends meet. Maybe you hate looking in the mirror. Or your connections with friends and family are mediocre. Perhaps you're always on edge, forgetting something really important, or never doing enough. I totally get that. It wasn't until I started making a plan that I began to alleviate a lot of very similar concerns in my own life. I woke up unimpressed with where I was in life, constantly having the feeling like I was forgetting something extremely important even though I wasn't, on edge because I thought I should be doing more or maybe less. I had a mild sense of paranoia about where I was in life and where I thought I should be. I started having trouble sleeping, which then made me more anxious because I knew sleep was extremely important. I wasn't working out enough. I wasn't eating the way I should. It started bleeding into my interactions with others, and I wasn't connecting with friends and family the way I should. I was living at the poverty line, and I was twenty-eight years old. I was not okay with all this. Why couldn't I be motivated to do my workouts or tackle simple tasks throughout the day? And why couldn't I even get motivated to get out of bed?

Everything changed when I had something to strive for. It changed when I started defining myself based on where I wanted to be and not where I currently was. I felt I had a great deal of untapped potential, and so I began making a plan to chase after that. And nothing has been the same since. I wanted to develop a real plan to actualize my potential—and it all boiled down to how I defined myself. When I decided I wanted *desperately* to become a Green Beret, I tried my hardest to behave like one. My whole journey—my training before joining the Army, selection, and then the Q Course—was possible because I now had an identity to strive for. Once I identified who I wanted to be, I was able to stay focused on the actions that were required to achieve my goals.

Exercise: Visualization

Set a timer on your phone for five minutes and imagine what your perfect life would look and feel like. Close your eyes and imagine your life five years from now when everything is going exactly the way you've always dreamed it would. Picture yourself having time to enjoy the hobbies you love. Imagine feeling fulfilled in the job you've always wanted. See yourself surrounded by and spending quality time with the people who mean the most to you. Imagine looking at yourself in the mirror and being absolutely stoked by what you see. Picture yourself free from anxiety or depression and living a purposeful and fulfilling life. Now imagine the feelings associated with this dream life: excitement, contentment, satisfaction, peace, and so on. Dig into those feelings. Let yourself experience those emotions as if that future life is in the present.

Now, as you're still feeling those emotions, and you still have those pictures in your mind, write out present tense "I am" statements that represent that future life. The kind of future you really want is rooted in the kind of person you want to become. In the space below, write out the kind of person you want to be, *but write it in the present tense*. Don't write goals. Goals are things you want to achieve that are external to you. Instead, write out an identity—the kind of person you strive to become. Here are some examples:

- I am curious about the world around me and constantly seek out new information.
- I am the calmest one in the room, and people find safety in my ability to navigate my emotions.
- I am the epitome of physical health and am able to pursue any activity that piques my interest.
- I am dependable, loyal, and I create safe environments in which my loved ones thrive.
- I am financially independent and am able to enjoy all the experiences life has to offer without stress or anxiety.

Mental:

_____

_____

_____

Emotional:

_____

_____

_____

Physical:

_____

_____

_____

Social:

_____

_____

_____

Financial:

_____

_____

_____

Now that you have your identity statements, spend a few minutes every day reading them out loud to yourself. Replace the story you may have been telling yourself with the story you want to create for your life. It all begins with the kind of person you want to be.

Recommended Reading

The Untethered Soul by Michael Singer

Becoming Supernatural by Joe Dispenza

CHAPTER 3

Become the Most Interesting Person You Know

"What is the fruit of these teachings? Only the most beautiful and proper harvest of the truly educated—tranquility, fearlessness, and freedom. We must not trust the masses who say only the free can be educated, but rather the lovers of wisdom who say only the educated are free."

–Epictetus, Discourses 2.1.31-2.3a[4]

The Zen of "Fuck It"

I know some of you are seriously offended by cursing or vulgar language, but hear me out. There are two words that have been pretty substantial in regard to me pushing past my comfort zone, exploring new things, and taking necessary risks… or even not-so-necessary risks.

"Fuck it." This two-word combination might be the most liberating, powerful, and Zen-filled combo in the English language. "Fuck it" is the epitome of acknowledging most things are out of our control, but some things are very much in our control. "Fuck it" is, in its essence, the verbal expression of the understanding that life is very temporary. Not only temporary but fragile. So, how does one find the balance between experiencing as much as life has to offer while also being keenly aware of its temporary nature? By not living in fear. By embracing the mortality we all share and by knowing there

---

[4] Holiday, Ryan, and Stephen Hanselman, *The Daily Stoic: 366 Meditations on Wisdom, Perseverance, and the Art of Living*, 10.

is a great deal out of our control. We have the freedom to begin to experience things in a new way.

So where does "fuck it" come in? It's a verbal cue to yourself to acknowledge that the way ahead may be unknown, but fear will not prevent you from living. "Fuck it" is the acceptance of potential negative consequences because the risk has been weighed against the reward and deemed acceptable. "Fuck it" has sent me down black diamond ski slopes on my second day learning how to ski (full disclosure: I did more tumbling than skiing on that day). "Fuck it" has taken me bungee jumping. "Fuck it" has allowed me to rip it down the Autobahn in Germany on my Kawasaki Ninja. "Fuck it" has given me the confidence to leave the Army after ten years and start my own business. "Fuck it" has also gotten me in some trouble due to a miscalculation of risk. But in life, you never fail. You win, or you learn. "Fuck it" needs to be more readily accessible in your brain. It shouldn't be your default setting, but it should be in your toolbox and well-maintained.

Who's the Coolest Guy You Know?

After I graduated from the Special Forces Qualification Course, my first team was in Germany. And it was on that team that I met probably some of the best dudes I've ever worked with in my life. For whatever reason, one of them, Travis, and I just clicked and often hung out and discussed the future and potential business plans. I remember driving down the Autobahn in his busted-up Subaru, and he looked over at me and said, "Hey dude, who is the coolest, most interesting person you personally know?" I thought for a minute but couldn't really come up with an answer. I told him I didn't know. And he said, "If the answer isn't you, then you're doing something wrong with your life." And from that point on, he and I started a competition between the two of us to see who would be the most interesting man. Admittedly, he's kicking my butt right now, but I'm going to give him a run for his money.

So, what's the point of the story? The point is that we often look up to celebrities or even people in our own circle because they've done things or achieved things, or maybe we see their Instagram reels and we're like, "Man, that is so cool. What they achieve is awesome. I wish I could be like that." But I think we should be our own heroes. We should be the ones who are like, man, I'm so stoked about my own life. I'm so stoked by the things I've accomplished and all the things I hope to accomplish in the near future. The competition Travis and I now have about who is the most interesting man is fun because it constantly pushes us to try to achieve not necessarily huge things in life, but interesting things.

Microwavable Society

Why do we struggle as a society to be interesting? I attribute a lot of it to the easy access we have to entertainment and the resulting dopamine highs. Binge-watching TV on Netflix or Hulu and scrolling through social media are, for sure, culprits in this. It requires precisely zero effort to be entertained. Watching hours and hours of a TV show entertains you, yes, but it doesn't require anything of you.

You can just sit there and passively receive. Same with social media. Everything is easy to access. Everything is available right now. I can go on Amazon and order just about anything, and it'll show up on my doorstep in a day or two. We live in an almost microwavable society where everything is at our fingertips, is very fast, and requires very little of us. Don't get me wrong—I'm a capitalist through and through, and I support businesses improving systems to get things to you faster. But I think the downside to that is that we are getting soft, for lack of a better term, and as a result, boring. I think that because we're so used to things being at our fingertips and at our disposal almost immediately, it's getting us very used to not pursuing things that require effort. If we don't get immediate results, we skip it and say it's not worth it. I tend to disagree with that whole sentiment. In my personal life, I've found that the things that are most worthwhile require a great deal of effort, a great deal of energy, and a great deal of time. When I enlisted in the Army, I desperately wanted to be a Green Beret, and I was fortunate enough to be given the opportunity to try out. I got through selection, and I remember the day I was told that I passed; they said, "Now you have the opportunity to go through the Q Course." I was thrilled, but I didn't realize how long the Q Course was. My orders to become a medic tacked on an extra year, so I was in the Q Course for three years. Every single day, I had to wake up and choose over and over to pursue this thing I was desperately trying to achieve—that funny-looking green hat.

But to me, it meant a great deal because becoming a Green Beret would be the culmination of years of effort, blood, sweat, and tears. I think being exposed to things that are constantly at your fingertips and being too used to having that kind of instant access has started to dissuade us from pursuing things that require a great deal of time, energy, effort, and long-term planning. Again, the Q Course for me was three years long and was worth every minute of it because, at the end of the day, I was able to achieve something I set out to do, but it took a great deal of mental fortitude. Okay, I'm off my soapbox now.

Jack-of-All-Trades

So, back to becoming the most interesting person. "Jack-of-all-trades, master of none." That's a quote we've all heard, but it's really only half of the quote. The real quote is, "Jack-of-all-trades, master of none, is often better than a master of one." I find that super interesting because people who are really good at a lot of different things often get that first quote thrown in their faces. In actuality, if you've only mastered one particular thing, it limits your horizons. It boxes you in, and you can really only discuss or talk about a single topic in depth. Whereas somebody who's explored a great deal of different things and has read a bunch of different books on a bunch of different topics tends to have a little bit more ability to interact with people in different environments. They can also connect diverse experiences in interesting ways.

The mind loves to make connections, and it's through these connections that the information is really solidified. So, if you're really good in one particular discipline, but you're exploring others, your brain is automatically trying to connect the multiple disciplines in some way. When you find those connections, it helps solidify the information you've learned. That's why when you read a how-to speed-reading book—and I've read a couple of them—they suggest pre-reading or skimming text prior to going through and reading the assigned chapters. The reason behind it is that as you're pre-reading or skimming, your brain is picking up on keywords. Those keywords have already made a little connection in your brain, so when you go back to reread it, that connection is solidified, and the information is more thoroughly stored in your mind.

I love reading. If you'd like a reading list, I've got piles and piles of suggestions I would love to give you. Additionally, each chapter includes a couple of recommendations based on the chapter. As much as I love reading, the majority of the books I consume now are in audio form. I know there are some folks out there who scoff at audiobooks, thinking it's cheating. But I think they're great because you can learn while you're sitting in your car instead of listening to the radio. People also think you won't retain as much information if you're just listening to it. I disagree. I read a few articles a while back stating that information retained through audio versus text is pretty comparable. Whether you listen to a book or read a book, you're going to retain about the same amount of information. Additionally, Indiana Public Media reported on a study that found the same areas of the brain are stimulated whether listening to or reading a book.[5] According to the report:

---

[5] Clare, V. (n.d.), "Audiobooks vs. books in the brain," *A Moment of Science* (Indiana Public Media), https://indianapublicmedia.org/amomentofscience/audiobooks-vs-books-in-the-brain.php.

> "To the researchers' surprise, they found that there was no difference between what cognitive and emotional parts of the brain were stimulated whether participants read or listened to the same story."[6]

An interesting commonality I found between the two is that if I'm reading a text, I can remember what part of the page it was on, like top right or bottom left or something like that. And when I'm listening to an audiobook, if I think back to recall a particular segment that I was listening to, I remember where I was driving at that particular moment. That's because the brain is really good at remembering locations.

If you're interested in memory techniques, look up the loci method. "Loci" is the plural of locus, meaning position, point, or place. Developed in ancient Greece, the loci method is a way to memorize by associating the thing you're trying to remember with a place. Joshua Foer's book *Moonwalking with Einstein* does a great job explaining this technique. In fact, as Foer was doing research for the book, he put the techniques to the test by entering the U.S. Memory Championship in 2006. He ended up winning the title in his first year competing.[7] That was a fun little tidbit; you're welcome.

Get Awesome at Stuff as Fast as You Can

Okay, so what's my recommendation then? How do you become more interesting? First and foremost, be willing to try a bunch of different things. But the original gangster way to learn stuff is to consume and digest material.

I read another article years ago saying that if you read three books on any subject, you could be considered an expert compared to the general population.[8] The statistic they gave—and I don't know if this is an actual

---

[6] Clare, V. (n.d.), "Audiobooks vs. books in the brain," *A Moment of Science* (Indiana Public Media), https://indianapublicmedia.org/amomentofscience/audiobooks-vs-books-in-the-brain.php.

[7] Foer, J., *Moonwalking with Einstein: The Art and Science of Remembering Everything* (Penguin, 2012), 159.

[8] Mohajer, S., *The 3 Book Rule to Become an Expert,* September 19, 2019, https://siamohajer.com/the-3-book-rule-of-being-an-expert/.

statistic or a hyperbole—was if you read three books on any subject, you're considered an expert compared to 95 percent of the general population.

Now, I do want to make a distinction here. Reading three books on nuclear fission might make you more educated than 95 percent of the general population on that topic, but you are not an expert compared to people who have actually studied that for years and work in a nuclear power plant. There's a difference between considering yourself an expert compared to the general population versus the people who devoted years in a field to master a particular subject.

All right, so let's break down some numbers. If reading three books will make you an expert compared to the general population, what would that look like over the course of a year? Reading twenty pages a day will get you through a 300-page book in about two weeks. At that pace, you could read more than twenty books a year. And as we've discussed, reading three books effectively makes you an expert compared to the general population. Imagine reading twenty books on a subject. At that point, you could probably teach a course on it. And that's just in one year. Imagine doing that for three years. You could probably debate college professors on the topic!

What if you just wanted to be more well-rounded, kind of like that jack-of-all-trades I mentioned earlier. Imagine becoming more or less an expert on almost seven different subjects over the course of a year. You would become the person everyone calls for advice. You'd become the person that everyone wants to be around at parties because you can intelligently hold a conversation about a bunch of different things. Twenty pages a day will completely change your mental state. And, as just mentioned, it will probably affect your social life too.

But what about the time commitment? "Chris, I'm a slow reader; it'll probably take me thirty or forty-five minutes to read twenty pages." I want to offer you this—thirty to forty-five minutes is really only 2 to 3 percent of your day. So, are you willing to dedicate 2 to 3 percent of your day to becoming the most interesting man or woman you know? Now, this is just referring to reading. But nowadays—with things like Khan Academy and Udemy and even YouTube—there's so much information out there that you can make serious strides toward whatever subject you want to know more about. There's no excuse for not pursuing and learning all the things you want to.

Author and entrepreneur Jesse Itzler has a similar theory regarding general skill acquisition. He states that if you devote 100 hours of intentional practice or study toward a discipline over the course of a year, you will be better than 95 percent of the general population at that discipline.[9]

Scan the QR code for Jesse Itzler's *How to master any skill with the 100 hour rule*

The most interesting thing about this particular statistic is that when broken down over the course of a year, 100 hours is only eighteen minutes per day. The main thing to know is that with consistent effort, even if that effort is a relatively minimal time commitment, great things can be achieved. With a time commitment of about 1 percent of your day, who might you become?

The reason I bring that up is I don't want you to feel limited. Maybe you hate reading. That's okay. It wasn't until I was in college that I actually learned to like to read. When I was growing up, my dad required my sister and me to read thirty minutes a day during summer vacation. It was an absolute chore, and I hated every minute of it. I didn't even remember what I was reading. I watched the clock the whole time. It wasn't until college that I actually learned to love the knowledge I found in books. In fact, it was on my trip to Maui. Spending five weeks on a tropical island in the middle of summer sounds

---

[9] Sigma Habits, *How to master any skill with the 100 hour rule - Jesse Itzler Motivation* (YouTube, May 4, 2023), https://www.youtube.com/watch?v=sF9I2H9k0Ms.

great, but if you don't have a place to stay, the weather can be... well, hot. During my time on the island, I often slept on the beach, camped in the mountains, or occasionally stayed in hostels. I even spent a few nights sleeping in my rental car (the cops didn't appreciate that). Throughout the day, I had to find things to occupy my time. Spending all day on the beach and playing in the ocean was great, but eventually, I had to find places to cool off. It became a practice of mine to drive to bookstores during the hottest part of the day and spend a few hours walking around and soaking up the air conditioning. Incidentally, when walking around bookstores, there's not much to look at other than books, and I started finding some that piqued my interest, ranging from *Beowulf* to *Peter Pan*. As a result, I not only fell in love with bookstores, but I fell in love with reading, and it became a habit that's continued until today.

However, if you really hate reading—you really just can't stand it—there are so many resources out there to help you become an expert at all kinds of different things. I mentioned Khan Academy, Udemy, and YouTube already, but there are also podcasts and even TikTok and Instagram can be excellent resources when navigated intentionally.

So, there's really no excuse to not know how to do something. Maybe you need to figure out how to change the oil in your car, build a house, wire a house, or set up some kind of experiment for a science fair project. Whatever it is, there's plenty of material out there. It just requires you to stop scrolling through social media and stop watching TV all day and pursue it.

One Percent Improvement

I want to talk a little bit about a statistic mentioned in *Atomic Habits* by James Clear. A 1 percent improvement daily means that after a year, you're thirty-seven times better than when you first started.[10] Well, how do you measure that 1 percent improvement? And what does it look like? There are

---

[10] Clear, J., *Atomic habits: An Easy & Proven Way to Build Good Habits & Break Bad Ones* (Penguin).

certain areas in your life where a 1 percent improvement can be easily measured because numbers are heavily involved. Think about your bank account. With a 1 percent improvement every day, you can watch the numbers go up and adjust as needed to ensure that you're making that 1 percent improvement. It's the same with weight training progress. You can record all of your lifts and how much weight was involved. Based on that, you can calculate what the 1 percent improvement would be daily.

Other areas can be a little bit more difficult to quantify. For those, the 1 percent improvement daily becomes more of a metaphor. You have to be comfortable taking a look at your life and asking yourself how do I get 1 percent better every day in the emotional area of my life? I think that's kind of difficult to measure. In that case, you can track practices that lead you to daily improvement. I mentioned meditation. You may not be able to clearly track improvement in your ability to focus or keep control over your emotions, but you can track and record the practices that will lead to that improvement. You can tally how many days a week you meditate and for how long. Then, you can calculate a 1 percent improvement in those practices. For example, if you meditate for fifteen minutes on Monday, a 1 percent increase would be an additional nine seconds on Tuesday. Maybe that's not how you want to measure improvement, though. Maybe it's as simple as journaling your thoughts after meditation, with the intent to become more acclimated to the practice daily, until fifteen minutes becomes easy, and you increase to twenty minutes. Or maybe you can count how many times you've lost your temper lately and then try to get 1 percent better every day. The intent behind the 1 percent rule is to strive for an accumulation of continuous small improvements. Some things are easier to measure than others, so you may have to get creative with how you track that progress.

Ultimately, my recommendation is to take a look at your life as a whole and then constantly strive for a little bit more, whatever that may be, every day. You might wonder what you can start to pursue. What is it that you can do? And the answer is sort of up to you. If you want to get really good at day trading, start researching it and get really intense and intentional about day trading. Or maybe you've always had a fascination with World War II aircraft. Well, I'm sure there are a bazillion videos out there on YouTube or even TikTok where you could find out more about stuff like that. Everything can be easily learned. It just requires time, commitment, and effort.

What's the Next Mountain?

This whole process may seem a bit overwhelming, so let me tell you a quick story about how to adjust your mindset to ensure you're comfortable chasing after new things and things you want to learn and get better at. Back in 2018, Travis and I decided we were going to climb Mount Kilimanjaro. Kilimanjaro is not a very technical climb—you weren't roped in, and you didn't have to use ice picks. It was a steady hike the whole time. The reason is that you're working with guides who are constantly telling you, "Pole. Pole." Which means "Slowly. Slowly." The guides know you can succumb to altitude sickness if you go too fast. They tell you to go slow to make sure you get to the top. Eventually, you reach base camp, which is the camp right before you summit. You get there in the afternoon or evening and then begin climbing at midnight to reach the summit by sunrise (watching the sunrise at the top of the world is spectacular).

I remember Travis and I sitting together after we reached base camp. We were chatting and sipping our coffee, and across the base camp, this guy started yelling and screaming. I looked over and saw he had both hands over his head. The medic in me kind of perked up and wondered if he was okay. It turned out he was just really excited, and he was fist-pumping and cheering. "I did it," he was yelling. "I climbed Kilimanjaro!" He was in the crew that had summited that morning, and he had just come down.

Travis and I looked at each other and chuckled because he and I were already discussing what the next "mountain" was going to be in our lives. We were already seeking out the next adventure, the next thing we were going to pursue to challenge us, despite the fact that we hadn't even finished this particular mountain, this particular challenge. I think the lesson to learn from that is threefold. One, be present; enjoy where you are in whatever journey you're on, and look around and enjoy the view. Two, to ensure a greater likelihood of success, slow and steady will trump fast and sporadic. And three, never stop seeking out that next thing. Never stop seeking out that next adventure, that next challenge, that next mountain to climb. When we start getting super comfortable with the achievements and accomplishments we've already had, that's when we get really content with sitting down and watching TV all day and scrolling social media. You have to create a sense of urgency to constantly seek out that next adventure in life because that's what's going to make you the most interesting person.

Exercise: Jimmy Fallon Test

This exercise has to do with that conversation Travis and I had in his car on the Autobahn. How do you become the most interesting person? I call this exercise the "Jimmy Fallon Test." Pretend you're invited onto a late-night show to talk to the host—whether it's Jimmy Fallon or anyone else—and your goal is to be the most interesting guest they've ever had. What does that look like? What steps do you need to take to become their most interesting guest? The way I envision it, Jimmy stumbles across the fact that I was in the Army. I want my response to be, "Oh yeah, I was a Green Beret, but that was years ago." I want the mindset to be that I achieved that goal, but that wasn't where I peaked. It wasn't the end of my story. It was just a chapter in the book of my life. My goal is to have done a great number of other things that were worth talking about and worth discussing on a late-night show. I encourage you to do the Jimmy Fallon test. Take fifteen minutes right now and pretend you're going to be a guest on a late-night show and figure out what it would take to make you the most interesting guest. Then, start writing down all the things you've always wanted to pursue. Maybe it's hang-gliding, skydiving, or scuba diving. Or maybe it's being Mr. Olympia. Maybe it's writing a book. Maybe it's being an internationally famous public speaker. Maybe you want to end homelessness in your city. List ten things you've always wanted to do, and then start figuring out what it would take to start that journey. What's the first step you need to take to begin pursuing those things, and what will it take to improve by 1 percent every day?

1._____ 6._____

2._____ 7._____

3._____ 8._____

4._____ 9._____

5._____ 10._____

Recommended Reading

The Setup by Dan Bilzarian

Any Jack Reacher novel by Lee Child

CHAPTER 4

You Should Be the Calmest One in the Room

"When you start to lose your temper, remember: There's nothing manly about rage. It's courtesy and kindness that define a human being—and a man. That's who possesses strength and nerves and guts, not the angry whiners. To react like that brings you closer to impassivity—and so to strength. Pain is the opposite of strength, and so is anger. Both are things we suffer from, and yield to."

–Marcus Aurelius, Meditations 11.18.9b[11]

One of the Greatest Compliments

I want to tell you about one of the greatest compliments I have ever received. My team and I went to Texas because we were getting ready to deploy to Afghanistan in the next month or two. It was a big training event where we were doing various exercises and "raids" and things like that, and we worked very closely with some infantry guys there. It was kind of a miserable experience. We all got COVID, but we survived. Anyway, one evening, we were prepping for a "raid." We got all our gear ready, and we were hanging out with the infantry guys who would be rolling with us to the objective. We take off in a helicopter and fly to the objective about 15 or 20 minutes away. Once we land, we do a head count and make sure everyone has

---

[11] Aurelius, M., *Meditations: A New Translation* (Modern Library, 2003), 154.

all their equipment and nothing has fallen off or been left behind in the helicopter. We give the thumbs up, the birds take off, and we begin maneuvering into position so we can prepare to take down this village of bad guys we would be engaging. In training, we were not shooting real bullets at each other, just "sim" rounds, but it was to simulate how we would take down this particular compound. The first half of the team pushed up and started going from building to building. Then, the second half of the team pushed up and did the same. We were maybe thirty minutes into taking over this small village and I got a call over the radio: "Hey, we need a medic in this building." When I got there and stepped inside, there was a medical scenario set up, and the guy who was grading me on what I do was the medical officer for our company. I had my aid bag with me, and I was working alongside a PJ or an Air Force pararescue guy, Andre, who was great. We started working on the casualty—it was something simple like a gunshot wound in the leg. Andre and I checked his vitals, put the tourniquet on, and started bandaging him up.

About that time, two more guys burst through the door, and they're "hurt" too. Andre and I started to triage these guys, organizing them in order of importance and then treating them. We go to each guy and check for injuries and figure out how to treat them. Andre and I are working out of two aid bags, and we've got three injured we were dealing with. Then two more injured guys stumbled into the room. We were starting to run out of room and supplies. And then two more guys needing medical attention came in.

We were up to seven or eight people in this small room. I had some infantry guys keep the doors and windows shut and pull security to keep this collection point safe. Andre and I are just going around very methodically to each patient, going through our sequence: check this guy, fix him, and move on to the next one. And once everybody was essentially stable, we didn't stop. We continued our rounds, checking on each one and checking the interventions we had done to ensure that they were holding on.

I remember one of the last guys they brought into the room. I didn't see a visible injury on him, so I sat him down and said, "Hey man, can you talk to me?" He was having trouble talking, so I cut open his blouse to do an examination of his torso. When I opened it up, there were fake guts hanging out of his stomach, intestines everywhere. That's when he started spitting up fake blood. I thought, *Come on, man, this is not what I want to deal with right now*, but I started dealing with his injuries and patching him up.

The scenario continued to get more intense as the night progressed. We had a ton of people and not enough equipment to take care of everyone adequately. I knew we were going to have to get out of there, so I talked to the team sergeant. "Hey man, we need a medevac like yesterday. Can you make it happen?" He got the bird to land pretty close, and then we started organizing who was going to leave when. We moved those with the most serious injuries first. The infantry guys carried them out on litters to the bird. And that's when they called "EndEx" (End Exercise). The training scenario was over, and we were graded. I was emotionally spent at that point and pretty stressed out. But the compliment came the next day.

We were training again with some of the infantry guys and headed toward the training compound in the van, where we were going to work on close-quarters battle (CQB) stuff. One of the infantry guys looked over at me and said, "Hey man, can I ask you a question? How did you stay so calm last night?" Apparently, he had been one of the security guys I put on the door to keep the room safe. He told me he was watching Andre and me work through the injured, and from his perspective, it looked as though we were very cool, calm, and collected. He said he would have been freaking out and overwhelmed with so many injured to manage. I definitely took that as a compliment. I was like, all right, sweet.

Afterward, I thought about it and tried to come up with an answer as to where calmness comes from. I think it's threefold. It's confidence, control, and stress threshold.

Confidence

Confidence is an intimate understanding of one's capability. It's understanding very clearly what you're able to do and what you're not. Confidence typically comes from a great deal of training.

In other words, it takes a lot of practice. And so, looking back at the situation that Andre and I were navigating, I don't know if we appeared confident—I was a little stressed out at the moment—but we knew what we had to do for each patient.

I was taught a formula during my medical training: **MARCH**. It stands for **Massive hemorrhage, Airway, Respiration, Circulation,** and **Hypothermia** or **Head trauma**. That's the sequence we were to use to address situations involving an injured individual, and it's set up in such a way that the most important—the M, the **massive hemorrhage**—comes first because that's what will kill the fastest.

So, you fix that first and then move on to the **airway** and make sure it's clear.

Next is **respiration**—now that you have an open airway, are they breathing well?

Then **circulation**—is their blood pumping to all the areas of the body it needs to?

Hypothermia comes at the tail end. How do I warm them up if they've lost a lot of blood and are getting chilly now? So, MARCH is a checklist used to assess a patient's severity of injury and then figure out exactly how to navigate through all possible injuries.

I drilled that exact formula over and over during the special operations combat medic course. I was confident I knew each step in the formula because I had practiced it hundreds and hundreds of times. And so that's where a great deal of my confidence in the above scenario came from. I didn't have to try and think about what the next step was—I just knew it.

Control

I think the next element of being calm is being in control. And this one is actually the easiest one because what do you really have control over? The answer is very little. The only things one truly has control over are one's own thoughts and actions. Some people will argue, "Chris, you don't have control over your thoughts. I can't control what pops into my head!" Maybe so, but you are absolutely in charge of what stays there and what you choose to focus on. If you can control your thoughts and not let them get away from you, you then have the ability to logically make your next move as opposed to responding and reacting to negative or overwhelming thoughts. And ultimately, that is the goal.

Going back to the scenario above, it was overwhelming to have to deal with all those patients. But if I had let that sense of overwhelm take hold, I wouldn't have been any good to anybody. So, I focused on what I did have control over, and that was the next step in the formula.

Stress Threshold

The third part of remaining calm is your stress threshold. I'll tell you a quick story. My oldest daughter started driving this past year, and I was absolutely stoked. I was the one who took her out driving while she had her learner's permit, and I went out with her often because I wanted her to be successful. I wanted her to be trained up.

She and I have an inside joke about how her driver's training began while playing *Grand Theft Auto* years ago. We would take turns on the game—whenever I died, I would hand the controller to her, and whenever she died, she would hand it back to me. Her favorite part of the whole game was finding a cool car, getting inside, turning the radio to the station she liked, and then obeying all traffic laws in the game. She would play for an hour just driving around and listening to the radio, and I would be falling asleep, waiting for my turn. Fast forward to when she finally got her license last year. Again, I was stoked, but we were getting a little bit of pushback from her mom.

Maybe her mom didn't trust my ability to train our daughter because she wanted her to take some more driving courses. My daughter was getting kind of frustrated about this, but I explained to her that our stress thresholds are a little bit different. I used to jump out of airplanes and blow things up, and that was like normal office work for me. Therefore, what I consider dangerous is a little bit different from what her mom thinks is dangerous. Her mom has not jumped out of an airplane and, to my knowledge, has not blown anything up, so her stress threshold is a little bit lower than mine. When thinking about my daughter driving, yes, I'm concerned. I want her to be safe, but there are a lot of other, more dangerous things out there. Because my wife hasn't been exposed to those kinds of stressful situations, the idea of our daughter driving kind of freaked her out. I'm happy to say that my daughter has been driving very safely for several months now, so no issues there.

The Navy SEALs have a term that I really like, and it's called "stress inoculation." They do things like tie recruits' hands and feet together and then toss them into the deep end of a pool. Now, I don't recommend that you try something like that, but there are other things you can do that will incrementally and consistently expose your mind and body to stressful situations to expand your stress threshold. Some examples are very high-intensity workouts, cold plunges (this can produce a physiological as well as a mental response), sauna sessions (they can be stress-inducing in a positive way), public speaking, or martial arts (like jiu-jitsu). These are all stressful things that, when done in a controlled environment and exposed to them regularly, will expand your stress threshold and improve your ability to respond to other stressful situations. Intentional exposure to mental stress prepares you for when you experience a chaotic event in everyday life. Stress is no longer this brand-new phenomenon that you're trying to navigate but rather something you're used to, enabling you to keep calm and move past it quickly.

So, going back to the situation in the mass casualty scenario… why was I able to stay calm? Well, I was very confident in my ability because I'd had very extensive training. I was able to control my emotions because I had a formula to follow, regardless of what kind of chaos stumbled through the door. And due to the nature of my job and the training I had received, my stress threshold was relatively high, and I was able to manage the situation.

Exercise: Stress Inoculation

For this exercise, come up with a menu of intentionally stressful things you can begin to expose yourself to. Examples might be taking a public speaking or martial arts class, cold exposure (it's become pretty popular lately), high-intensity workouts, and sauna sessions. For me, striking up conversations with strangers at the coffee shop is stressful (I'm a bit of an introvert). Before engaging in any potentially stressful physical activities, consult your physician to be sure it's safe for you to participate in those. List out all your options below.

_____

_____

_____

_____

_____

_____

_____

Now, commit to doing at least one of the things you listed per week. As you grow accustomed to the activities, increase the frequency until you're engaging in at least one stress-inoculating activity per day. Keep this list fresh—over time, you'll have to change it up and think of new activities to engage in.

Don't Think. Do.

The MARCH formula described above was really just a checklist, a series of tried-and-true non-negotiables proven to solve the majority of problems you may face in a medical situation. The beauty of having this formula is that it takes second-guessing out of the equation. I didn't have to think about what to do next. I *knew* what to do next, regardless of who walked in the door. Not everybody was bleeding, so then I could move on to the next step. Could he talk to me? All right, his airway is clear. Is he breathing well? Is he freaking out? Yeah, he seems to be okay. How's his circulation? Kind of cool and clammy. Maybe he's got some internal stuff I can't see right now. Whatever the case was, that formula gave me the tools to successfully manage that large group of people.

Following a checklist works great *if* you follow the checklist. You start getting a little off the rails when you have a checklist and then deviate from it unnecessarily. Sometimes, the situation might dictate a different approach, but more often than not, if you can just stick to the formula and follow it as you practice it in a stress-free environment, then you're good to go. The checklist was created in a logical manner in a time of low stress so that it can be implemented regardless of the situation. Pilots do this for takeoff and landing, and they even have checklists to follow in emergency situations. Surgeons in hospitals started implementing checklists to ensure the safety of patients. During my medical training, I had the opportunity to work in some hospitals and participate in various procedures. During surgeries, there is a very specific way of doing everything. And they do it that way *every single time* so that everybody knows their role. They account for all of the equipment and tools used during the surgery so that nothing gets left behind in a person.

Checklists are ideal for high-stress environments and situations, but they also work great on a day-to-day basis when dealing with normal stuff. Make a checklist or a to-do list the night before a potentially stressful event, and then, when you go to implement it the next day, don't think; just do.

"But Chris," you might say, "I have trouble focusing long enough to come up with a good checklist." I'm glad you brought that up.

It's Called Practice for a Reason

Let's talk about meditating. I'm a firm believer that meditation eventually becomes a superpower. The ability to stay focused in a culture of distraction will set you apart. "But Chris, I could never meditate. I can't sit still long enough to do that." That's like saying you're too dirty to take a shower. Meditation takes practice, a lot of practice. "Chris, I don't have time to just sit there and be quiet." I read a quote from Dr. Sukhraj Dhillon a long time ago, and it goes like this: "You should sit in meditation for twenty minutes a day unless you're too busy. Then you should sit for an hour."[12] Think of it as a workout for your brain. There's a common misconception about meditating. Maybe you eventually get to the place where you totally empty your mind, but you definitely don't start out there. Often, the meditation practice you engage in (and one that I really enjoy) is simply sitting still and taking some deep breaths, focusing on each one. And then, as your mind begins to wander and chase a thought down whatever rabbit hole, the practice is to bring yourself and your attention back to your breath. I don't think the goal is to empty your mind. I think that's really difficult. But the goal is to be aware of your thoughts as they show up and then to gently bring yourself back to the point of focus, which might be your breath or a mantra you're repeating. If, in the span of fifteen minutes, you become aware that your mind is wandering and can bring yourself back to your breath a thousand times, that's a successful practice

---

[12] Coach, E.G.-. T. S. M. a. Y. E., *Best morning routine tips and tricks your kids will actually follow* (April 26, 2023), https://www.linkedin.com/pulse/best-morning-routine-tips-tricks-your-kids-actually-emma-g-.

because you were aware of your thoughts and could bring yourself back to the point of focus.

Okay, so meditation helps you focus on things because it's intentionally practicing being present and dialing in on a singular thought for a certain amount of time. The practice I engage in most frequently is the one described above, where you sit quietly and focus on your breath or a mantra, and every time your thoughts begin to wander, you bring yourself back. But there are a lot of different meditation methods out there, and you need to find one that works for you. When I discuss with clients the process of beginning a meditation practice, if their ultimate goal is to be able to meditate for thirty minutes, I usually don't encourage them to start out with a full thirty minutes because it's exhausting and difficult if you're new to meditation. Often, I'll encourage them to begin with maybe sixty or ninety seconds of bringing their thoughts back to the point of focus and then work up to more extended periods. It's just like any kind of practice. If somebody's brand-new to the gym, I wouldn't expect them to be able to bench press 315 pounds if they've never done it before. So go easy on yourself and cut yourself some slack in regard to meditating.

This ties into what was discussed earlier in the chapter regarding the three components of maintaining calm: confidence, control, and stress threshold. Meditating directly relates to the control aspect of calmness. Learning to be aware of your thoughts is the first step in learning to control them and your emotions. As mentioned above, it's hard to control the thoughts that pop into your head, but a consistent meditation practice trains you to be aware of those thoughts and how to refocus after a thought begins to wander. Think of how well you'd be able to manage your emotional state if you had control over the thoughts that led to various emotions.

And please don't hear what I'm not saying. I'm not encouraging anybody to behave like Spock from *Star Trek*. We don't want to be so logical that we're devoid of emotion. Rather, I encourage you to feel all of your emotions. But you should be in charge of those emotions and not let them dictate your next step. Moments of regret are often the result of responding emotionally to a situation. Have you ever yelled at someone because they said or did something and then regretted it later? That's because emotions are temporary. And temporary feelings shouldn't elicit responses that have permanent effects on your life. How many relationships have been permanently damaged because someone "lost their temper?"

Regularly engaging in meditation helps reduce those moments of regret by training you to respond the way you *actually* want in any given situation. It gives you the tools to become aware of your thoughts and emotions and refocus on the thoughts you want. This creates a little bit of a buffer between you and the situation, and sometimes, that moment or pause before a response is all that is needed to prevent a potentially damaging interaction.

One of the clients I work with puts it this way: there is a space between the stimulus of the situation and one's reaction. Learning to capitalize on that space is where potentially chaotic situations can be defused. There's a technique I learned during a particularly uncomfortable training phase in the Special Forces Qualification Course. When asked a question or when presented with a stress-inducing statement or situation, you should pause, breathe, think, and respond. I want to take this a step further, though. Practice this technique *all the time* because calmness is required during times of chaos, and you don't want to practice it during those times. If you engage in this technique all the time, it will become second nature, and you'll naturally do it when you actually need it. So when having a conversation with someone, pause, breathe, and think before responding. It takes less than a second. And if you practice this often, it'll be readily available to you in those high-stress moments.

Exercise: Pause, Breathe, Think and Respond

Begin using the technique listed above in all of your conversations today. In the next conversation you have with someone, even if it's a pleasant chat that doesn't induce any stressful emotions, pause, breathe, think, and then respond. Repetition is key. And just like anything new, it will feel uncomfortable at first, and that's okay. Do it anyway. After that conversation, come back to this chapter and write down your thoughts on how that conversation went. Was it weird? Pleasant? Did the other person even notice? Did you begin to feel that space between stimulus and reaction?

_____

_____

_____

_____

_____

_____

_____

Exercise: Meditation

You didn't really think I was going to talk about meditation and not have you practice, did you? You should have known better! I want you to try this—and no cheating, no skipping to the next chapter. This won't take very long. Set a timer on your phone for two minutes. After I describe what you need to do, then you can start your timer. You can either sit up or lie down. Take three deep breaths in through your nose and release them through your mouth. Take deep breaths, and feel your belly expand. After your three breaths, breathe in for a four-count, hold for a four-count, breathe out for a four-count, then hold for a four-count. Breathe in, two, three, four. Hold, two, three, four. Breathe out, two, three, four. Hold, two, three, four. That's one round, and we are going to do eight rounds. That'll be about two minutes, or stop when your timer goes off.

Something that helps me is focusing on where I feel the breath. Sometimes, I feel it in my chest, and I notice my chest expanding and contracting. Other times, I focus on feeling the air come in through my nose and dial in on that sensation. Or if you just want to focus on the count, that's totally fine, too. If your mind wanders in these two minutes, that's okay. As you notice stray thoughts, gently bring your focus back to the breath. Be kind to yourself. Don't be harsh. Gently refocus and keep going. Ready? Go.

How was it? Write down your thoughts here. Did you enjoy it? How do you feel now? Was it uncomfortable? When your mind wandered, were you gently bringing your focus back to the breath?

_____

_____

_____

_____

_____

_____

_____

Now, I want you to commit to doing that once a day for at least two weeks. I promise you can find the time to devote two minutes a day to developing this skill. Once you're able to focus for two minutes, begin increasing the duration or the frequency in which you engage in your practice. You got this!

Recommended Reading

The Daily Stoic by Ryan Holiday
*The Subtle Art of Not Giving a F*ck* by Mark Manson

CHAPTER 5

"Show Me Your Friends and I'll Show You Your Future"[13]

"Some people are sharp and others dull; some are raised in a better environment, others in worse, the latter, having inferior habits and nurture, will require more by way of proof and careful instruction to master these teachings and to be formed by them—in the same way that bodies in a bad state must be given a great deal of care when perfect health is sought."

–Musonius Rufus, Lectures, 1.1.33-1.3.1-3[14]

Quit Hanging Around Bums (QR code-Dan Pena on YouTube: explicit language warning) The title for this chapter is from Dan Pena, and if you know Dan Pena, you either love him or hate him. He's probably one of my favorite people to watch on YouTube because he has absolutely zero filter. He's going to tell you exactly what's on his mind, and he's not going to sugarcoat it at all. And I like that. But that quote has stuck with me for a long time because it's 100 percent accurate. The people you allow into your inner circle, the people you allow into your life, are incredibly influential on the trajectory of your overall life.

---

[13] *Show me your Friends...* (n.d.) YouTube, retrieved March 10, 2024, https://www.youtube.com/shorts/-zb5EDa5af0.
[14] Holiday, Ryan, and Stephen Hanselman, *The Daily Stoic: 366 Meditations on Wisdom, Perseverance, and the Art of Living*, 225.

And we very rarely take that into account. Often, when growing up in school or even beyond school in the workplace, your friend group is kind of forced upon you because that's just who you're around all the time.

But in my experience, I think a better practice would be to be very selective with your friend group. You don't have to be rude to people. You can be kind to everybody, but be as selective of who you allow into your tribe as you would be with the kinds of food you put into your body or the kind of training regimen you engage in (and maybe some of you need to be more selective about that, too). Because the people you surround yourself with play a vital role in how you move forward.

Iron Sharpens Iron

There's a verse in the Bible that says, "As iron sharpens iron, so one person sharpens another" (Proverbs 27:17).[15] I think this is spot on. When I was in the Army and serving on Operational Detachment Alphas (ODAs), I was constantly surrounded by incredibly high-caliber people. In a previous chapter, we talked about being an expert compared to the general population versus an expert in a specific field. I would argue that when I was a Green Beret, I was probably in the top 10 percent of the general population in terms of my physical ability. But compared to the guys I worked with, I was average. I was constantly surrounded by people who were pushing themselves—not only physically but mentally—in all areas.

So, what did that do for me? It forced me to want to measure up to their standard. It forced me to want to push myself in all areas. I wanted to be smarter just by being around them. I wanted to be kinder because these guys were essentially my brothers. I wanted to be stronger, faster, and more physically capable. I didn't want to be the weakest link on the team. And maybe that performance paranoia—always wondering if you're doing enough, always wondering if you're going to measure up to the standard that's been set—is a good thing. If the standards that you and your friend group

---

[15] Proverbs 27:17 (NIV), Bible Gateway, https://www.biblegateway.com/passage/?search=Proverbs%2027%3A17&version=NIV.

have set are super low, then yes, you're constantly achieving that standard, but you're not progressing. You're not moving forward. Being around high-caliber people for so long has ingrained into my brain that pursuing excellence in all areas is vital and necessary and needs to happen. Before the Army, I worked out a lot, but most of that was just out of fear that I wasn't going to make it through selection. But after the Army, after spending years with guys for whom working out was a vital part of their lives, I feel like a complete dirtbag if I don't work out every day. I don't have anyone standing over me, making me hit the gym, but it's now an essential, non-negotiable part of my life. The legacy left from being around the best dudes on the planet has had a lasting effect on how I conduct my day-to-day life.

Once I decided to step away from my Army career to pursue full-time mindset coaching, I had to reconcile that walking away from that tribe was going to be the most difficult part—and it has been. Since leaving the Army, I've had to be incredibly intentional with who I allow into my inner circle and my tribe. The good thing about that is I get to pick and choose who I allow to have influence over where I'm moving in life. The downside to that is those people are few and far between, and they often don't live in my town, so connecting with them requires intentional phone calls or reaching out in other kinds of ways.

The people who surround you can sharpen your edge and make you better, but you have to ensure that the people you allow into that circle, into your sphere of influence, are high-caliber people who are going to make you better. Part of my coaching practice and what I do now has to do with accountability. Accountability is a buzzword that's thrown around quite a bit, but what does it mean? The definition is "a state of being liable or answerable." My question is, answerable to whom? What I tell everybody I work with is that your progress is your responsibility. You are really only accountable to yourself. And this may sound like it's running counter to what I just said about the friends in your life and the people who have influence over you, but I'll get to that in a second. Ultimately, your progress, the direction you're heading in life, and the pace at which you're progressing are entirely your responsibility because only you can do the work to make it happen.

You might be different from me, but I have found that if I make a commitment to myself, it's typically the first thing that gets put on the back burner when life happens. When something with the kids comes up, or when somebody has an emergency and needs help moving a refrigerator—whatever it is that I had planned for me usually gets postponed or canceled. So why is this? Why this sense of accountability to others? Well, when I tell somebody else that I'm going to do something, I make a commitment to them. As a result, I have found that those commitments get done on time, and they get done well.

And so, yes, ultimately, you are accountable only to you. It's your responsibility to move forward. But having people around you who will hold you to those commitments, or at least ask you about them, helps in the follow-through.

The Cost of Oversleeping

I want to tell you a quick story. One of my oldest friends, Brad, and I have known each other for twenty-plus years. He's a solid guy, and he's one of those guys I'd call if I needed to hide a body in the middle of the night. He's been there forever, and I trust him with everything. Well, a couple of years ago, I wanted to start waking up earlier—to better own my morning and set my day right—and I decided to get up at 5 a.m. every day. For a while, I would set my alarm, and as soon as that alarm went off in the morning, I'd hit snooze multiple times, and for about an hour and a half, I wouldn't get up. I didn't follow through on the commitment I made to myself. I soon realized I needed some help. I called Brad and said, "Hey man, this is what's going to happen. I'm going to set my alarm tomorrow. And if you don't get a text message from me proving that I'm up, awake, and doing things, I'm going to Venmo you $100." If I sleep through my alarm, he gets $100. If I get up, he knows that I'm following through on the things that I want to do. I had struggled with waking up for months—I would set the alarm and just hit snooze over and over and over again. But as soon as I implemented this little tactic, I was up on time and ready to go.

After a while, I didn't even need the alarm. I was waking up at 4:30 because I was almost too scared to oversleep, knowing I'd have to pay. Fast forward a little bit to several months later. The process had been working great, but I stayed up too late one night and wound up sleeping through my alarm. In my groggy state, I had hit the off button when the alarm sounded. A couple of minutes later, my eyes popped open. I realized it was ten after five, and I'd missed my deadline. And so I texted Brad to let him know $100 was coming his way—he was pumped.

At that point, I decided to make it $500. If I overslept, Brad would get $500. So, what's the takeaway from this? What's the lesson? If the joy of doing your tasks does not outweigh the joy of putting them off, then you need to make the pain of *not* doing them greater than the pain of doing them. In my case, the joy of staying warm under the covers was greater than the joy of getting out of bed, so I had to make the pain greater. As I've mentioned before, it's your responsibility to move forward. Your life is entirely your responsibility, but it can sometimes be beneficial to ask for support when you need it. The trick is to surround yourself with the right kind of people.

In the Unlikely Event the Cabin Loses Pressure

A principle I want to drive home is that you should be making sure that you're measuring up to the standards you set for yourself and the people closest to you. An analogy I use often in my coaching practice is that of the oxygen mask. When you're flying somewhere, before you take off, the flight attendants tell you that if cabin pressure is lost, oxygen masks will drop, and you should be sure to put on yours *first* and then help those around you. I use this analogy because that is the best way to navigate through life. For me to help the people around me, the friends I've allowed into my circle, and be of better service to them, I need to be firing on all eight cylinders and moving forward in all areas of my own life in the best way possible. One of my favorite philosophers, Ayn Rand, has a book called *The Virtue of Selfishness*, in which she discusses this kind of principle. The title is kind of funny, and I think she did it on purpose to provoke some conversation. But in *The Virtue of Selfishness*, she talks about not sacrificing your own well-being to the point of death to help people you're not invested in.

I know that sounds horrible, but hear me out. Sacrificing your own growth and progress in order to perpetually aid those around you, particularly those you don't consider part of your tribe, is not the best approach. It will leave you burned out and less capable of helping others down the road. Please don't hear what I'm not saying. I think helping others is incredibly important and should be done often. My point is that if you are sacrificing sleep, or not eating, or neglecting your physical fitness or emotional well-being just to *do more* for others, you will eventually run out of fuel and have to stop.

The best way to help the people around you, even people you don't know and have no real connection with or ties to, is to make sure you are physically, mentally, and emotionally healthy and are progressing in such a way that you have the ability to influence all of those people in a positive way. That then spreads further than just your inner circle because when you are performing better in your own life, it raises the standard of your inner tribe, which then has an impact on their sphere of influence, and so on and so forth. The better you are at progressing forward, the more positive impact you can have on not only your inner circle but the world at large.

A Community of Consequence

Your next question might be, how do I find a community? How do I find a group of people who will hold me to the standard of continual improvement? How do I find what I like to call a "community of consequence?" Well, it all starts with *you*. You may have noticed that this has been a recurring theme throughout these pages. Your friends, the people you allow into your inner tribe, should expect a lot from you. And they should be genuinely surprised when you don't measure up to the standard that you have set for yourself. So, I think a better question is, how do I *build* that community? As mentioned before, it begins with *you*. You have to become the kind of person you would want in your community. I recall somebody talking about relationships a while back, and the topic was how do I find my dream person, the person I want to spend the rest of my life with? The same philosophy applies here as well—it all begins with you becoming the kind of person you would want to date.

Being kind and caring, physically fit, financially stable, and mentally acute—all of these things begin with you. You have to start to become the type of person you want to spend the rest of your life with. I think that applies to building a community, too. To attract the sort of people that you would want to help influence the trajectory of your life, you have to be the kind of person you would want in your tribe. As mentioned earlier in the book, you have to pursue things that make you more interesting and more intelligent. You have to make physical fitness a big part of your life and an important factor in moving forward. You have to become emotionally intelligent and be calmer in stressful situations.

How does this process begin? How do you become that kind of person? It begins with some serious self-reflection. You have to start asking yourself what areas you need to improve. Where are you falling short, and what can you really dial in to improve your overall performance in all areas of life? Going back to one of the earlier chapters, this relies pretty heavily on identity and the kind of person you want to become. The kind of individual you want to be should dictate your daily habits and actions—and that includes the kinds of people that you want to associate with and be around.

For example, the identity I strive for in the social realm of my life is being the anchor for my friends and family. What I mean by that is I want to be the one who is stable enough for them to cling to for support and safety through whatever storm in life shows up. Here's a funny story regarding this: When I was telling one of my earlier clients the identity I'm striving for, he kind of chuckled because he referred to his mother as the anchor of their family, but for a very different reason, primarily because she was always dragging everyone down.

The next question you might have about the process is, what should you look for in a tribe? What should you look for in the people you want to surround yourself with? I'm going to give you a couple of key factors that I would associate with the kind of people you allow into your inner circle. I've used a phrase for years now: "Real friends stab you in the face." What that means is that the kind of people you want in your tribe are the kind who aren't going to talk poorly about you behind your back.

Instead, when they have an issue with you, they will sit down in front of you and say, "Hey man, you're not measuring up," and point out what you did that was out of line or inappropriate. You want them to be able to come to you and tell you face-to-face what the problem is. If they're talking about you behind your back but are all smiles to your face, that's not a good sign. For that to happen, you have to create an environment in which it's safe to have that conversation with you. If every time someone comes to you with an area in which you're not measuring up, you blow up and lose your mind and freak out at them, they will be less likely to do that in the future, which is not what you want. What you want is for them to come to you often and say, "Hey, maybe you can do better in this area. How can we move forward?" But again, that requires a great deal of effort on your part to ensure that the environment is safe enough for the people in your life to approach you.

After Action Review

In the Army, after any training event, mission, or exercise you'd do as a team, you'd perform an After Action Review (AAR). It was a simple process where everyone in the group had to contribute three "sustains" (three things we did well) and three "improves" (three things we need to do better). It's an excellent way to review how things went and fix or establish standard operating procedures. It could get uncomfortable sometimes if you made some mistakes and people were talking about them, but the intent was to make the team better in the future.

On my first team, there were a few of us who were always striving to grow as individuals and teammates. Chris, Travis, and I were constantly talking about the future, including potential business ideas, new workout plans, and new adventures to go on that would challenge us. One day, we decided to begin conducting weekly AARs on each other. Once a week, we would bring our lunch to the team room, sit at a table, and take turns offering "sustains" and "improves" to each other. No one was exempt, and you had to offer at least one of each. These "sustains" and "improves" weren't limited to job performance but included all areas of life. For example, "Hey man, your workout routine is awesome—keep crushing it," or "Dude, what was the last book you read? What are you doing to grow your mind?" Admittedly, the first couple of meetings were a little awkward because even as close as we were, we weren't used to giving personal critiques like that. Eventually, though, those meetings became something we craved because it was an opportunity to grow, and the suggestions came from people we trusted thoroughly.

Exercise: After Action Review

List two or three people you'd be willing to conduct an AAR with. Now, actually do it! What were the "sustains" and "improves" the others gave you? List them below. Remember that "sustains" are things you should keep doing, and "improves" are things you need to work on. It will be awkward at first, but if you can do this regularly, you'll learn to look forward to these meetings.

People to have AAR with:

_____

_____

_____

Sustains:

_____

_____

_____

_____

Improves:

_____

_____

_____

_____

There are a few other attributes that you should look for in your friends and the people in your inner circle. The **first** would be that they're absolutely thrilled when you experience success or have a victory in your life. They should be stoked and cheering with you—and not the fake cheering where they're secretly pissed off and upset that you're experiencing a victory.

The **second** would be that when you experience loss, they are genuinely sorry. They grieve with you and experience that pain with you, as opposed to secretly cheering the fact that you just had a major setback or loss. If the people in your life are secretly cheering about your loss, they aren't the ones you want in your circle.

The **third** attribute is that the members of your tribe are genuinely surprised when you don't measure up to the standard that you've set for yourself. If all of you as a group have set pretty high standards for yourselves, and then you don't measure up, all of them should be like, "Whoa, what just happened? What's going on? Is everything all right?" If they're not surprised, that means they expected you to fail, and that should be a warning sign and a topic for discussion.

To reiterate, there are specific attributes you should look for when adding people to your circle. They should celebrate with you when you experience success. They should grieve with you when you experience loss or a setback. They should be surprised when you don't measure up to the standard you've set for yourself.

Dude, Buy an Xbox

So, now what? You now need to be very intentional about connecting with the people you've allowed into the inner circle of your life. I think a face-to-face, in-person connection is always a little bit better than something occurring over the phone, but sometimes all you have is the phone. My buddy Brad lives in Virginia, and I'm in Colorado. I remember when I was just starting my coaching business, he was begging me to buy an Xbox so we could play video games together. After putting it off for months and months and listening to him pestering me constantly, I finally relented and bought an Xbox. I'm not a gamer, and I'm not very good at it, but what buying that Xbox has actually done is allowed us to now connect multiple times a week. We talk over a headset and get to hang out and discuss business while we're shooting the bad guys.

If you're spread out location-wise from your circle, it's important to find ways to close the distance, and you can get pretty creative with doing that. But you should not only be intentional with making an effort to connect with the people in your life and having specific times to reach out to them, but you should also be intentional with what you talk to them about.

The Good Ole Days

I had a friend (another Green Beret) when I was in Germany, and I remember I had to drive him up to Landstuhl, a medical facility in Germany. He had to get some work done. While I was driving him there (and it was like a two-hour ride), he was telling me all these great stories about when he was in high school and college and the stuff he'd done in the past. After he had his work done, I drove him back the next day. And he, again, was talking my ear off, mostly about things he had achieved and accomplished in the past.

I bring this up because you need to be intentional about the things you talk about with your close friends. If all you ever do is reminisce and talk about the good old days, I think an adjustment needs to be made. A better way to approach it would be to make plans for the future. Tell me what it is that you're pursuing now in physical fitness or business. Tell me how your family is and what you're planning to do to maintain the connection with your wife and kids moving forward. That type of thing. So not only is it important to be intentional about connecting with your inner circle, but it's also important to connect about specific things—and I would highly recommend forward-thinking things. Again, it's totally fine and totally appropriate to occasionally talk about the good old days and times past. But if that's all you ever do, if all you're ever doing is living in the past with your inner circle, an adjustment has to be made. So again, forward thinking. Strive to plan where you want to be moving.

Another thing I'd recommend in regard to finding solid people in your life is to find a mentor, somebody who's way far ahead of wherever it is that you are to learn from. It's important to have peers, people who are sort of on the same level as you. And I think it's important to have somebody that *you* can mentor. But having a mentor, somebody who's maybe a little bit older, or at least further down the path than you are, is important because now you can glean all of the wisdom they gained from mistakes they made that you would like to avoid and learn what it is that made them successful or got them to where they are. Learning from someone else is a vital part of the growing process.

I think it's incredibly important to have peers. They are vital in moving you forward in the way I mentioned earlier (iron sharpens iron). But having someone to mentor lets you help someone else avoid some of the mistakes you've made. You might say, "But Chris, I'm not an expert at anything. How can I mentor someone else?" You don't have to be an expert to help. You have an entire life's worth of experience. Sharing that with someone who isn't as far along on the journey is a good practice to engage in. I think that dynamic is huge because when you teach something, it's also a learning process. You solidify some of that knowledge even more so in your mind as you're teaching it. Having someone ask you questions that maybe you hadn't thought about before gets you thinking in a different way—and maybe that helps you avoid other mistakes in the future. So again, find a mentor, surround yourself with peers who are on the same path as you, and then find somebody you can mentor.

Exercise: Community of Consequence

For this exercise, take a few minutes and list all of the qualities you would want in a circle of close friends. Write down the non-negotiable qualities you want in the people you spend your time with. Additionally, take a couple of minutes and write out the qualities you absolutely *don't* want in your circle. It's okay to include things that would be deal-breakers.

Non-negotiables:

_____

_____

_____

_____

DealBreakers:

_____

_____

_____

_____

Next, make a list of people you know or want to know who exemplify the non-negotiables you listed above.

_____

_____

_____

_____

Now, here comes the hard part. Write down all the ways *you* are exemplifying the qualities you're looking for. Remember, creating the right kind of tribe begins with you.

_____

_____

_____

_____

Recommended Reading

Fire in the Dark by Jack Donovan
Never Split the Difference by Chris Voss

CHAPTER 6

Look Good Naked and Be Hard to Kill

"At dawn, when you have trouble getting out of bed, tell yourself: 'I have to go to work—as a human being. What do I have to complain of, if I'm going to do what I was born for—the things I was brought into the world to do? Or is this what I was created for? To huddle under the blankets and stay warm?'"
—Marcus Aurelius, Meditations 5.1[16]

The title of this chapter is one of the personal identity statements in the physical realm of my life. I want to look good naked and be hard to kill. Some of that is left over from the Army—the hard-to-kill part. But the looking-good-naked part, I think, rings true. And as funny as it may sound, if you are happy with what you see when you look in the mirror, if you're pleased with the state of your physique, that's a testament to your daily habits and actions over the course of years of your life. If you're not satisfied with what you see in the mirror, it's also a testament to your daily habits and actions over the course of your life. So, if you want to change something, it's going to require a change in daily habits and actions. Now, the hard-to-kill part, again, is sort of just funny and left over from Army life because being hard to kill is kind of part of the job. But I think there's still some truth to it. There have been studies showing that increased muscle mass helps prevent fatalities in car accidents and that type of thing. The healthier you are, and the more in shape you are—

---

[16] Aurelius, M., *Meditations: A New Translation* (Modern Library, 2003), 53.

eating healthy foods and exercising in a way that helps your heart, lungs, and muscle tone—the harder it is for life to take you out.

A Box of Dunkin' Donuts a Day

Calories in versus calories out. I won't lie; the guys on my team used to hate me because every morning when I came into the office, I would bring a large box of Dunkin' Donuts Munchkins for the guys to snack on. They would all glare at me while they grabbed a couple, telling me I was going to make them fat. I just laughed because I've always known it's calories in versus calories out. I'm not a nutritionist, but I'm pretty good at math. Your body simply existing and not doing anything else will burn a certain number of calories throughout the day.

Let's just say that's 2000 calories. If you want to lose weight, you need to consume less than you're burning or burn more than you're consuming. Before anyone freaks out at me, always consult a physician prior to engaging in a new diet to be sure it's safe to do so. If you're trying to lose weight and just existing every day without doing much more, you're burning 2000 calories. If you want to lose weight, lower your consumption to 1700 or 1800 calories, and you will start to drop weight. The same with increasing your weight. If you want to put weight on, you're going to have to consume more calories than you're burning (I'll tell you a story about that shortly). There's a phrase in the fitness realm: "abs are made in the kitchen." I believe that. We might see all the fitness models on Instagram, and their abs are just popping out everywhere. Well, that's primarily because their diet has allowed them to shed fat to expose the abdominal muscles on their body. If you have a surplus of mass around your midsection, that's because your diet isn't appropriately proportional to your workout. And again, it goes back to the calories in, calories out.

Sometimes I talk to people who are absolutely thrilled with the progress they've made in losing weight—they started a new diet and have essentially become evangelists for whatever that diet is. I think diets begin to work primarily because it's probably one of the first times you've actually started to pay attention to the food going into your body. And that's an important thing to take away because if we're more intentional with the food we eat, we'll probably start to hit some of our weight goals moving forward. It likely has less to do with following one specific diet or another. It's more about calories in versus calories out.

Pass the Twinkies

Mark Haub was a professor of human nutrition at Kansas State University. He did an experiment for ten weeks about counting calories and how that is most important in regard to losing or gaining weight. In the experiment, he ate Twinkies, Ding Dongs, Doritos chips, and Oreos. He wanted to prove that he could lose weight. According to the CNN article, he was able to lose twenty-seven pounds over the course of ten weeks.[17] You're all probably thinking that he's likely almost dead as a result of all the junk he put in his system. Well, according to Haub, his bad cholesterol, or his LDL, dropped by about 20 percent, and his good cholesterol increased by 20 percent. His triglycerides also decreased by 39 percent. So what's the takeaway then? According to the CNN article, "Haub limited himself to less than 1,800 calories a day. A man of Haub's pre-dieting size usually consumes about 2,600 calories daily. So he followed a basic principle of weight loss: He consumed significantly fewer calories than he burned."

This was just one study (done by one man), and I think it goes back to my point that weight management is really calorie management. Having said that, I'm curious how he was feeling throughout this ten-week experiment. The kinds of fuel you put in your body are important to performance. Yes, maybe he was able to lose a lot of weight, and certain levels in his blood tests came back pretty good, but what was his performance like after that? For your Honda Civic to function properly, you put regular gasoline in it, and that's

---

[17] CNN, B. M. P. (n.d.), *Twinkie diet helps nutrition professor lose 27 pounds*, CNN.com, https://www.cnn.com/2010/HEALTH/11/08/twinkie.diet.professor/index.html.

fine, but if you want your Lamborghini to operate properly, you need to use the high-end stuff, the premium.

As you're starting to move forward and progress toward certain fitness or performance goals, start dialing in the kinds of food you put into your body. A person just starting out their fitness journey isn't going to perform in the Olympics right now. However, if you're an Olympic athlete or striving to become one, the kinds of foods and fuel you put in your body will help you perform in a certain kind of way. Now, full disclosure again: I'm not a nutritionist. But I do have certification as a personal trainer through the National Academy of Sports Medicine, and generally speaking, counting calories is one of the best ways to lose or gain weight.

The August Experiment

Let's talk about gaining weight now. Back in 2022, I conducted what I call the "August experiment" (I called it that because it was done throughout the month of August). The intent behind the experiment was to intentionally gain weight. My metabolism is pretty high, and even though I want to be a beefcake one day, I've always had trouble putting on the pounds. In the experiment, I was going to consume between 4,000 and 4,500 calories every single day—kind of like Haub's experiment in reverse. I didn't care where the calories came from. It could be a bunch of steak or a box of donuts. It didn't matter. As long as I was hitting my caloric intake, that's all I cared about.

As somebody who's kind of a hard gainer, I had never really been able to break 200 pounds and maintain it. Throughout the experiment, as I was consuming all of these calories, I was able not only to hit but maintain that 200-plus-pound body weight throughout the month. I didn't get fat—I just got bigger. And my performance levels didn't go down. I still weight-lifted constantly. However, I was tired all the time. When I think back on that fun little experiment, I remember being kind of sleepy a lot. Now, I have zero science to back this up—it's just my personal assumption—but I think I was tired a lot because much of my energy was probably going to digesting food.

So, what did I eat? Anything I could get my hands on. I tried to eat half-decent meals, but there were multiple days when I was getting ready to go to bed, and I realized I was short by maybe 1,000 to 1,500 calories. I'd look around and try to find something that I could slam really fast to add the calories I needed. Uncrustables, those pre-made peanut butter and jelly sandwiches, were a common grab for me (they're delicious, by the way). Depending on which ones you get, they can be about 300 calories a piece. I'd slam five or six of them to hit my calories for the day. And then I would go to sleep.

What did I learn from the experiment? Well, it confirmed what I preach to my guys all the time: that it's just calories in versus calories out. Whenever I'd bring in a box of donuts, they were pissed off at me, but the reality is that if you want to get bigger or smaller, you just have to adjust the number of calories you're bringing into your body.

Exercise: Calorie Audit

For the next two weeks, I want you to track the number of calories you put into your body every day. Don't worry about macros right now; just focus on total caloric intake. I'm not even asking you to change anything about your diet right now. Just track and annotate your calories every day. This will require a little bit of effort on your part. You'll actually have to look at food labels to get the information you need, primarily the number of calories in a serving, what constitutes a serving, and how many servings you consume. It'll take a couple of minutes per meal or snack. Don't forget that liquids have calories too. At the end of each week, you have space to calculate your daily average. To do that, add up all the totals for the first seven days, then divide by seven. That will be the first week's daily average. Repeat the process for the second week.

Again, no need to change your diet. This is just to get a baseline of what you're consuming on a daily basis. You can then do whatever you want with that information. *Start today!*

Day 1: _____   Day 8: _____

Day 2: _____   Day 9: _____

Day 3 _____   Day 10: _____

Day 4: _____   Day 11: _____

Day 5: _____   Day 12: _____

Day 6: _____   Day 13: _____

Day 7: _____   Day 14: _____

Average: _____   Average: _____

The Real Game Changer

Okay, so moving on to training. "Chris, how often do you train, and how long do you train?" I used to joke with people that I train nine hours a day. Their eyes would get really big, and they'd wonder how that was even possible. The joke was that I would train for about an hour in the gym and then sleep for eight hours. I think sleep is one of the most overlooked, under-prioritized functions of the body. Sleep is really where you make all of your gains. Not only physically, but if you're trying to retain the information you may have learned throughout the day, ensuring that you get quality sleep is vital for that process. I remember years ago, as a high schooler, I wished that there was a pill—and I guess there might be now—that would allow me to stay awake and never have to sleep.

I have since changed my perception and understand that sleep is so vital that I've changed my entire bedroom structure to ensure that I get high-quality sleep. Tracking things is one of the best ways to learn about what's going on in your life and in your body. The phrase I like to use is "what gets measured gets managed." For years, I used a sleep tracker app on my phone. It's called, you guessed it, *Sleep Tracker*. It measures the number of hours you sleep and the different sleep cycles. I have since upgraded to a different sleep tracker (and I'm not sponsored by this company—I just think it's a really cool product). I bought the Oura Ring, which tracks sleep cycles and also measures resting heart rate while you're asleep. It measures SPO2, which is how well your blood is carrying oxygen throughout your body, whether or not you're stirring throughout the night, and how restful your sleep is.

I think it's important to keep track of data like this—and I'm a little bit of a nerd, so I like looking at numbers—because you start to notice patterns that develop in your life. The app associated with the Oura Ring is great because you can scroll through and look at not only today or last night's sleep, but pretty much every day for however long you've had the app. It does a great job of tracking the patterns of your sleep schedule, measuring what time you go to sleep, how long you've been asleep, how long you've spent in each sleep cycle, and all the other metrics I already mentioned.

Now, the importance of tracking data is to notice patterns and then adjust life accordingly to better optimize what it is you're trying to achieve. For example, I found that my resting heart rate at the time was in the low fifties throughout several weeks. That was essentially my baseline pattern. Although I'm not a big drinker, there were one or two nights where I had a beer late at night and then went to bed, and when I checked the data the next day, my resting heart rate was much higher, and my sleep wasn't as restful. I learned that alcohol disrupted my sleep pattern, even if I didn't necessarily notice it the next day. Now I try to avoid drinking late at night because I understand that it's going to disrupt my sleep pattern and sleep quality, which is then counteracting the physical or mental work I may have done earlier that day.

As I mentioned a second ago, I've changed my bedroom to better accommodate my sleeping patterns. I've made what I call the slumber cave. When it's nighttime, and I've finished my work for the day, my room is pitch black. I've got double blackout curtains over the windows to prevent any kind of ambient light from outside coming in. I try to keep my phone in a separate room if I can. I cover any kind of LED light from other electronics, like the air conditioner, with black tape, and I try to keep the room very cool between 66 and 67 degrees while I'm sleeping. I think some studies have shown that covering up with blankets and even wearing hoodies and sweatpants is totally fine, but the ambient air in the room should be cool. It should resemble a cave. And that's why I call it my "slumber cave," because it's pitch black and very cool.

I don't know about you, but I hate waking up to loud, jarring noises, but that's pretty much what all alarm clocks do. But I found one that simulates a sunrise. If I set my alarm for five or six, it starts getting brighter about thirty minutes prior to that, so by the time it's time to wake up, my brain has awakened naturally to light as opposed to sound, which is a much gentler way to wake up. And then I'm in a much better mood. Overall, it's been a significantly more pleasant experience.

There are some other things that the sleep specialists in the Army recommended. One is to make sure that the bed is only for sleeping. If you're sitting up watching TV in bed, that's a big no-no. Even when sitting up and reading in bed, your brain starts to associate the bed with something other than sleep. As I was getting out of the Army, I was having trouble sleeping. The recommendation was that rather than lying in bed, tossing and turning, I should get out of bed, go to a different room, do something boring, like read a textbook or something, and try to wind my mind back down before lying back down to sleep. Another tip that I found incredibly useful is to write down all those negative thoughts swirling about in my head when I'm trying to sleep to get them out of my head. What that does is sort of "trick" your brain into thinking that the problem has been solved, so you don't have to worry about it right now. It makes it a little bit easier to drift off to sleep. I do highly recommend tracking your sleep in some capacity, even if it's as simple as writing down when you go to bed and when you wake up in a journal. Ideally, you wake up and go to sleep at the same time every day. That's not always possible, but it's the best way to set your circadian rhythm and set you up for success for high-quality sleep.

You may have been thinking that this chapter was about physical fitness, but I haven't really talked about working out. It's all been about eating and sleeping. But I started out that way because both are such a vital part of the healing and recovery process that if they aren't prioritized, all the work you do in the gym isn't going to progress as quickly or as thoroughly as you want it to.

Exercise: Sleep Audit

I want you to track your sleep for two weeks. There are plenty of apps out there you can download to help you do that, and they will help with the accuracy of this exercise, but if you don't feel like using them, it'll be okay. What I want you to do is write down how many hours of sleep you actually got each night. Again, the apps that track your sleep will give you more accurate data because they can differentiate between lying in bed and actually sleeping, and they can also indicate the times you wake up throughout the night. Similar to the calorie audit, I want you to annotate your daily average at the end of each week. Add up all the hours you slept, then divide by seven. That's your average for week one. Repeat the process for week two. Remember that "what gets measured gets managed." As you track your sleep schedule, compare your average to the recommended sleep requirements put out by Sleepfoundation.org.

Day 1:_____hrs.   Day 8:_____hrs.

Day 2:_____hrs.   Day 9:_____hrs.

Day 3:_____hrs.   Day 10:_____hrs.

Day 4:_____hrs.   Day 11:_____hrs.

Day 5:_____hrs.   Day 12:_____hrs.

Day 6:_____hrs.   Day 13:_____hrs.

Day 7:_____hrs.   Day 14:_____hrs.

Average:_____   Average:_____

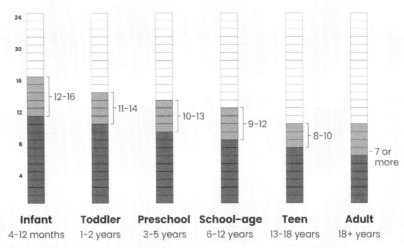

---

[18] Suni, E. & Suni, E., *How much sleep do you need?* (Sleep Foundation, January 3, 2024), https://www.sleepfoundation.org/how-sleep-works/how-much-sleep-do-we-really-need.

I'll Throw a Dodgeball at Your Face

Something I tell my clients often, particularly if they're just starting their fitness journey, is don't do something that you hate doing because you're not going to do it for very long. This may run counter to what a lot of fitness personalities say, but hear me out. I'm more interested in you engaging in physical activity that you'll continue to do for a long time rather than absolutely destroying yourself in the gym doing things you hate—and then quitting after a couple of weeks. Interestingly, I've found that as people progress on their fitness journey, different kinds of workouts become more appealing because their level of capability has increased. Imagine this scenario. You are a complete "couch potato," but you commit to walking every day. Eventually, you lose some weight, have more energy, and begin to feel more confident.

It's around this time that you ask yourself, *I wonder what I'm capable of?* So, on a whim, you sign up for a local 5k race, which motivates you to train a little harder. After the race, you want to really challenge yourself, so you research local marathons and sign up. All you cared about initially was finishing that first race, but now you want to see if you can improve your time, so you sign up for another. After four or five marathons, you're inspired to register for your first sprint triathlon. Now things are getting interesting. My point is this: Begin where you are. Do something you can do consistently. As capability increases, new opportunities become available and, more importantly, appealing.

Some folks love running, and I encourage them to go do it. I am not that guy. I hate running, so I get cardio in different ways. I definitely prefer the rowing machine over running. And I prefer jiu-jitsu over both of those. I think you see my point. Find something that you can do and do consistently.

When I was in the Army, group physical training (PT) events were often just long runs. And running is good cardio for sure, but man, it's boring, and I hate doing it. Whenever I was in charge of setting up group PT for the day, I would usually pick something fun like Ultimate Frisbee®. (You may call me a nerd, and that's totally fine, but I can throw a Frisbee® farther than you!) The reason I picked Ultimate Frisbee® is that in an hour of playing with a bunch of super-competitive Green Berets, you end up sprinting the entire time—chasing down the disc, playing defense, and trying to outrun and outpace everyone around you.

The added benefit is you're moving laterally as well as forward and back. When you're just going on a long run, your body gets really used to running in a straight line, whereas if you're doing something a little bit more dynamic, your body uses other muscles that help you dodge and move around in more than just a straight line.

I always pick something fun to do. If I enjoy doing it, then it makes me want to do it more. And just because something is fun doesn't mean it can't improve your fitness level. That's the takeaway. Fun does not equal wasted time. Do something you'll continue to do for the long haul. As you begin to see results from your consistency, start exploring other aspects of fitness that may interest you. If you hate running but you want to get outside and be active, hiking is a great option, or even just walking around the block. Walking is one of the most underrated exercises out there because we, as humans, are designed to move and walk for long distances. There are endless options: volleyball, pickleball, martial arts, freediving, calisthenics, rock climbing, competitive jump roping. Find the thing you enjoy—and do it often.

If you thought I was a nerd for playing Frisbee®, buckle up. Years ago, I was a youth pastor, and we would play dodgeball every single Sunday. I'd give a little message afterward, but dodgeball was my favorite thing. Throwing a ball as hard as you can at a middle schooler and then seeing him smile after you nailed him in the face is hilarious. And so, I have dodgeball in my blood.

When I was in Germany, we were doing team PT, and it was my day to choose the activity. It was probably raining outside, so we couldn't do Frisbee®. I was like, let's play dodgeball! I was able to convince not only my team but also the company commander, who was a major, and the company sergeant major to join us. Maybe this is a little mean, but there is something so satisfying when you, as a staff sergeant, are throwing a ball at a major as hard as you can, and there's nothing he can do about it. It always put a smile on my face. But it was also a great workout, and it got me moving. I was sprinting the whole time and moving my body in a way that forced me to be mobile and flexible.

So again, stick with a workout you find enjoyable. Find the thing that you can stay consistent with and do that over and over and over again. That's what will help you with your physical fitness journey. If you hate weight training, maybe don't do very much of it. I think weight training is incredibly healthy and important, and I always encourage it because it's just good for your body. Maybe you want to be a marathon runner. Well, that'll require a lot of running, but maybe that's what you enjoy. The trick, particularly when you're starting your fitness journey, is finding something that you love and can do consistently because that's what's going to carry you to the next phase where you want to try something a little more challenging. It's going to broaden your horizons and push you to explore avenues of fitness that you maybe haven't considered before. But if you're just starting out, the key is finding something you can do consistently and do often because you enjoy it.

Having said that, if you're just starting out, don't bite off more than you can chew. You know, sometimes, particularly at the start of a new year, people get super excited. They hit the gym and absolutely destroy themselves for like a week or two straight. And then they're so sore that they can barely function, and they start dreading going to the gym because now the brain is associating the gym with pain as opposed to enjoyment and growth. It becomes a mental block. And so again, if you're just starting out, I typically recommend that until you've been on this journey for a while, do just enough to where you are eager to hit that workout the next day and not so sore that you can't function and are miserable.

How Do I Start?

What's the next step? If you're just starting your fitness journey, I think step one is figuring out what your fitness goals are. If you want to be an absolute beefcake or Mr. Olympia, that's going to require a very different set of actions than being a triathlete or a marathon runner. In a later chapter, I'll provide an exercise for you to identify your goal and get really specific with it, and then I'll provide space for you to give yourself a deadline to accomplish it. If you're a beginner just get started and build that consistency.

If you're further along in your fitness journey, now it's time to really start dialing in your sleep and nutrition. The fastest gains are usually made when you're first starting out. If you're beginning to notice a plateau in performance, you really have to start paying attention to the little things to bust through those sticking points—not only the amount of recovery time you're giving yourself but also the quality of sleep and recovery. It's not just dialing in nutrition and fuel, but maybe getting more regimented with the times and the schedule to consume those fuels. For example, you might want to implement a window within which you consume caffeine. It's best to wait about ninety minutes after waking before slamming that first cup of coffee. And not consuming caffeine for six hours or so before sleep is ideal because it will disrupt your sleep, which will in turn disrupt your ability to capitalize on the work you did that day.

This whole book is about incremental improvement over long periods of time to achieve the kind of success you want in life. To achieve fitness levels that are in alignment with your potential, you must understand that you can't cram for fitness. You can't expect this to be a fast process. Additionally, you're never *done*. It's a lasting process that can always be adjusted, tweaked, and improved upon. To achieve the goals you're chasing after, your fitness journey must become part of your identity.

Exercise: Commitment

If you're just starting out, I want you to list one simple thing you can begin doing today and then commit to doing it *every day*. For example, "I commit to doing twenty pushups a day" or "I commit to walking for fifteen minutes a day." If, however, you're further along in your fitness journey, I want you to write down one thing you can begin to dial in better. For example, "I commit to tracking my sleep and making sure my sleep routine is adequate to give me the recovery I need to make the progress I want," or "I commit to tracking all of my macros and developing a meal plan that gives me the necessary nourishment to perform the way I want." You got this!

_____

_____

_____

_____

_____

_____

_____

Recommended Reading

High-Intensity Training the Mike Mentzer Way by Mike Mentzer

Jiu-Jitsu University by Saulo Ribeiro

CHAPTER 7

Wealth Doesn't Happen by Accident

"To accept it without arrogance, to let it go with indifference."
—Marcus Aurelius, Meditations 8.33[19]

Get Mad

I'm not a financial coach. I don't have a degree in finance or banking. What I do have is personal experience dealing with money. I went from having to go to the free clinic in town when I got sick, not being able to pay all my bills each month, and having to stay in friends' houses for free, to having a successful Army career for ten years, buying my own house, and eliminating all of my bad debt (student loans, car loans, credit card bills). I was able to do all of this when I made one mindset shift—I decided I was responsible for how my financial situation looked. And that's when I got pissed. I attacked my student loans like it was my job. I stopped being afraid of bills and shifted my frame of mind from one of fear to one of gratitude. Every time I paid a bill on time, I got stoked.

And that's a mindset I still have today, although most of my bills are auto-drafted from my bank account, so I don't even remember what days most of those things are paid. The point of this is to explain that a mindset shift needs to take place. I started telling myself I'm good with money. I started

---

[19] Aurelius, M., *Meditations: A New Translation* (Modern Library, 2003), 107.

telling myself that I'm actually really well off. I started telling myself that dealing with money is exciting because I have enough. And then I really started believing it.

An important point to mention is that when I realized my money was my responsibility, I wanted to get as smart as I could on the subject. I consumed as many books as I could on money and finances. And even if I've forgotten 90 percent of the material in those books, I'm still light years ahead of folks who choose not to educate themselves at all. When I accepted responsibility for my finances, I took it very seriously. I no longer wanted to scrape by or live paycheck to paycheck. I wanted to excel, so I laid out my plan to do just that. Remember that the goal of this book isn't to be better than everyone else—it's to be as good as *you* possibly can be.

Strawberry Milkshakes and The Catcher in the Rye

Back in 2006, between my junior and senior years of college, I decided I was either taking six weeks out of the summer and hitchhiking across America or potentially going somewhere more specific. Through some uncomfortable conversations with my dad, he convinced me not to hitchhike across America and encouraged me to pick a destination. I settled on Maui. I'm not sure exactly why I picked Maui other than I wanted to go somewhere tropical and enjoy the beach and that type of thing. As the summer approached, my dad asked if it was okay if he joined me for a little bit of that trip. So I flew to Maui with my dad, and we kind of bummed around the island for a couple of weeks together, did the tourist thing, and enjoyed all the beauty the island had to offer. We found a rental car company that rented out older vehicles and rented a busted-up Nissan that had no air conditioner and blended in well with the locals.

For the first couple of weeks of my trip, my dad and I played tourist. And then he flew back home, and I was on my own for another three or four weeks. That was an interesting time because I'm a little introverted, and I think I needed some help busting out of my shell back then. Anyway, I remember doing a lot of hiking and camping and sleeping on the beach, and I read a lot of books. I remember Dad and I walking through a market somewhere when a shirt caught my eye. It said, "There are two ways to get rich: earn more or require less." I absolutely loved it, and I remember that phrase well and think it's accurate. To become wealthy, whether in your own eyes or society's eyes, it's going to require you to make a lot of money, do something that has value, and provide it as a product or service to other people and increase your net worth that way. The other way is to be content with the simpler things in life and enjoy experiences rather than material things.

During that trip, I remember sitting in a mall. I had just ordered a strawberry milkshake from McDonald's, and it was getting kind of late. I wasn't quite sure where I was going to sleep that night—it was either find a hostel or sleep on the beach or in the back of the rental car. But I remember picking up my strawberry milkshake and grabbing the book I happened to be reading at the time, *Catcher in the Rye*. I walked out of the mall toward the rental car, trying to figure out what I was going to do that night, and I don't recall ever being so content. I was essentially homeless for a few weeks, but I felt really blessed because I had all the things I needed in the moment, which at the time was a strawberry milkshake from McDonald's and a decent book.

It's Not You, It's Me

The point of the story is to help you begin redefining your relationship with money and wealth. When I work with clients and we begin discussing money—more specifically, their financial goals—everyone has a different desired end state. Some want to retire early. Others want to become multimillionaires. Some want to buy their dream house, but others want just a small plot of land where they can get peace and quiet. The reason we go through this is to determine what kind of behaviors need to be adopted to achieve their goals. However, we must first get comfortable talking about, thinking about, and interacting with money.

Money is one of those things that is sometimes uncomfortable for people to talk about. Growing up, I just always assumed we didn't have any money, even though, looking back, there was no reason to think that. We weren't on the poverty line or anything like that. We had a roof over our heads and food to eat and we took a vacation every year. We were pretty middle class. But money was never discussed, and I think that was a bummer because it was a missed opportunity to teach my sisters and me how to be responsible with money.

Talking about money is one of those things people get kind of uncomfortable about, but I don't think it should be avoided because money is how you navigate through life. We exchange currency for products or services, and it's an important part of life. I think one of the better approaches toward money is Dave Ramsey's principles. I don't necessarily agree with everything he has to say, but I think what he gets absolutely right about money is that it's a psychological relationship.

One of his principles or "baby steps" is implementing the debt snowball. The idea behind the debt snowball is to list all of your "bad debt," from smallest balance to largest, regardless of the interest rate of each. Make the minimum monthly payments on everything except the smallest debt. Attack that one with as much ferocity and extra money as you can until it's eliminated.[20] Mathematically, it may make more sense to order your debts from highest interest rate to lowest, but what Ramsey understands is that humans make a lot of decisions emotionally. The following excerpt is why I think the debt snowball method works:

> "The quick wins you get with the debt snowball help you *believe* you can actually pay off your debt. And if you believe it, you'll start behaving like it. That's why it worked for me. Once I saw my smallest credit card debt get knocked out, I did a little happy dance (internally—you don't want

---

[20] Kamel, G., *How the Debt Snowball Method Works* (Ramsey Solutions, December 22, 2023), https://www.ramseysolutions.com/debt/how-the-debt-snowball-method-works.

to see me dance externally). And my brain was like, *That was awesome! Let's do it again!* That's the power of psychology—and the debt snowball." [21]

Getting quick wins does something to us emotionally. It keeps the fire lit beneath us and keeps us going for the long haul. It begins to build what I call "psychological momentum." That momentum increases as consistency is maintained. And that momentum, backed by consistency, develops into long-lasting behavioral changes.

And that's what this whole book is really about: developing behavioral changes that will bring about the growth and progress you're looking for in all areas of your life. If you don't like Ramsey's approach to money management, that's fine. I don't agree with everything he teaches, but he's definitely right when he says one's relationship with money will greatly influence how they interact with it.

Exercise: Money Relationship

Let's address your relationship with money. In the space below, write down your experience with money growing up. Was it a sore subject at home? Was it ever discussed? Do you have any idea if it was managed well? What are some poor habits you picked up regarding money? What are some great habits you picked up?

_____

_____

_____

_____

---

[21] Kamel, G., *How the Debt Snowball Method Works* (Ramsey Solutions, December 22, 2023), https://www.ramseysolutions.com/debt/how-the-debt-snowball-method-works.

What's your current relationship with money like? Does the word *money* invoke feelings of stress or anxiety, or is it a neutral topic? Is money something you manage well, or do you simply hope there's enough in your bank account each month? Do you use a budget? What are your current spending habits? Are you and your significant other on the same page about money? Do you ever argue about it? What are those arguments really about?

Now, I want you to describe the relationship with money you really want. Describe the feelings you want to have when discussing budgets and monthly spending. Do you want your finances to be well-organized, or do you even care? What do you want to be able to accomplish with money? Dig wells in Africa? Donate to the charities of your choice? Buy a yacht?

_____

_____

_____

_____

_____

_____

Now that you've spent some time digging into your past and present relationships with money, write down one behavior you will implement or change altogether to begin to ensure your future relationship with money as you envision it. For example, implementing a budget, having regular discussions about finances, stopping overspending, eliminating consumer debt, and so on. Commit to this new behavior for ninety days.

_____

_____

_____

_____

What Would You Do with a Brick?

Being wealthy or rich does not mean you're a bad person. I feel obligated to say this for a couple of reasons. First, this whole book is about striving for excellence in all areas of your life, including your financial situation. Second, some of you need to get over this weird mindset that rich equals evil. It doesn't. Money is neutral, and your relationship with it greatly influences the role it plays in your life. If you're obsessed with it, then it will probably affect the level of stress you're experiencing because you're always scared it'll leave. If you think it's an evil thing, you'll probably subconsciously try to avoid it. If, however, you learn to adopt the same emotional attachment to it as you would a hammer, then you will learn to love how useful it is when you need to drive a nail. But you probably don't tuck your hammer in at night and read bedtime stories to it. You probably keep it handy so it's available for use in the right job. And you probably don't think about it all day long unless you have a job that requires it.

Going back to Dave Ramsey, he has this cool thing that he teaches, and that is that money is amoral, meaning it doesn't have morals. Money is the equivalent of bricks. With a brick, you can do a lot of interesting things. You can build an orphanage or a hospital with it, or you can smash windows with it. Money is the same way. How that money is implemented and what kind of effect it's going to have on the people around it depends on who is wielding it. Money is an amplifier. It makes you more of who you already are. And that's why I think it's incredibly important to know exactly who you want to be *before* you get started on the path toward wealth and get a lot of money. So, going back to your financial identity, who do you want to be financially? I think that's an important question to ask.

Exercise: Financial Identity

Go back and review the financial identity you wrote down in Chapter Two's Visualization Exercise. Think about it. Does the identity you came up with accurately embody the kind of relationship you desire to have with money?

How's Your Foundation Looking?

Just like everything else talked about in this book, financial success is a process, and it requires certain behavioral changes. Depending on the goals or desires you have for your financial future, you'll need to begin adjusting behaviors to align with those goals. A bodybuilder's goals are different from a marathon runner's goals, and as a result, their daily habits and actions will look very different. Despite those differences, they may both be incredibly successful in their own eyes. That's something to keep in mind. Your financial journey is yours, not anyone else's. If those around you don't understand why you've started a side hustle and are living frugally in order to set up a nest egg, that means their goals are different from yours. Don't be dissuaded from taking the actions you need to achieve the success you want. You may look crazy in others' eyes, in the same way that bodybuilders may look crazy to marathoners. But that's okay. Keep doing the work that needs to be done.

If you started the necessary work ten or twenty years ago, and now you're cruising toward success, congratulations. If you haven't, stop sulking and start today. Nothing changes if no action is taken. As I've mentioned before, it helps immensely if you know what your desired end state is. Having a net worth in the top 10 percent of earners in the U.S. will require different habits and actions than building a cabin in the woods Thoreau-style. Both may lead to similar levels of personal satisfaction, but the path to each will look very different. It's up to you. The point is to figure out what you want and begin laying the foundation to achieve that goal.

Common Best Practices to Consider

1. **Learn to emotionally detach from money.** It's a tool you get to use, and you decide the best way to use it.
2. **Conduct an expense audit.** This is similar to a sleep audit or calorie audit. Just track all expenses for a month to see what you're spending your money on.
3. **Create a budget you can live with.** A budget tells your money what it should be doing. There are many options for this—assign every dollar a place to go or base your budget off percentages, i.e., 25 percent for rent or mortgage, 10 percent to savings, 2 percent for fun and extracurriculars, and so on.
4. **Create an emergency fund.** I have found when crises show up; they are less chaotic and stressful if I have a fund that can handle them. Things like a car breaking down or a water heater going out seem less like a crisis and more like a minor speed bump when I have the means to fix the problem.
5. **Begin educating yourself in the realm of finance.** There are a lot of great books and podcasts out there. If you are financially uneducated, begin learning today. Digest the material as though you actually care about your future.

Eleven Dollars a Day

Going back to what I was talking about with Dave Ramsey and how money is more of a psychological endeavor and relationship, I want to tell you a little bit about one of my first clients, John. John, who was down on his luck, had sort of been in and out of trouble with law enforcement for quite some time. When he came to me, it seemed as though this was kind of his last shot, his last resort to get his act together. I remember us going through the identity exercise and trying to figure out what it was that he wanted to be in all areas of life. When we got to financial, he gave me the identity that he wanted to have, and I was like, this is great. Then we got to the actual goal setting itself.

I asked him to tell me where he wanted to be financially in five years. He said he'd like to have maybe $5,000 in the bank.

I told him that wasn't big enough. Aim bigger. And I threw a number out there and said, "Why don't you strive for $20,000 saved up in the bank? I think that's a pretty solid goal, and it's bigger than what you're already aiming for." He didn't think there was any way he could ever do that. After consulting my calculator, I told John that $20,000 saved over the course of five years is only $11 a day, and I asked him if it was possible for him to deposit $11 into his savings account every day. The point of the story is that the big goals we may be chasing after are often easier to achieve than we might think. We just haven't taken the time to break them down and see what it would take if we put forth consistent effort every day. In John's case, it was only $11 a day, which is significantly easier to manage than thinking about $20k.

Sometimes we get super wrapped around the axle about a giant goal, but once we break it down, it's not as intimidating. It just takes consistent effort.

Storytime

I want to talk a little bit about how I think money is really a relational or psychological thing. When I joined the Army, I had a significant amount of student loan debt hanging over my head, and that was one of the reasons I wanted to join the Army. I wanted some financial security and stability so I could start paying down that debt.

When I went on active duty, I remember calling the loan company and explaining my situation. They were excited. They were like, "Oh, congratulations for joining the Army and becoming active duty. Tell you what, we won't make you pay a monthly payment. In fact, you can defer your payments until you get out of the service." I thought that was awesome. But what they didn't tell me was that I was still accruing interest on that principle the whole time I was in the Army. So, as my military career progressed, I had this rain cloud kind of looming in the back of my brain, saying, *Hey, you have this debt that needs to be dealt with. When are you going to do that?* I kept putting it off because the company had told me I didn't have to make monthly payments, but every time I looked at the balance, it got bigger and bigger because that interest was still there. Right around 2018, I got fed up with my lack of financial education and my lack of understanding of how money works.

I remember picking up just about any book I could get my hands on that dealt with money, whether it was on personal budgeting or investing or whatever. I read anything I could get my hands on and tried to digest the information. One of those books happened to be *Think and Grow Rich* by Napoleon Hill. I love that book because it taught me the power of visualizing the things I want and chasing after the things I deem important. As a result of reading that book, I found a financial affirmations audio track. It would say things like, "I'm really good with money, and I pay all my bills on time," and "I get joy from paying all of my bills."

Full disclosure: When I first started listening to the affirmations track, I thought it was the stupidest thing I'd ever heard in my life, but I stuck with it because I had just read *Think and Grow Rich*. I listened to the affirmations on my walk to work every morning, while I was in the office every day, and on my walk home—over and over and over again. After a couple of weeks, it didn't feel so dumb anymore. I got to the point where I was excited to listen. And then, after a few more weeks, I was like, you know what? Maybe I *am* good with money. Maybe I *do* take joy in paying my bills on time.

One day, something clicked. I was completely fed up with that student loan debt looming over my head. I went a little nuts and started throwing every spare dollar I could at the outstanding balance. I had a couple of motorcycles in Germany that I wound up selling, and what I got for those motorcycles went toward the balance. I became so obsessed with it that every time I paid a little bit on that debt, I took a screenshot of the new balance, and that became the lock screen on my phone. Every time I picked up my phone, I would see it and say, "All right, we're getting a little bit closer, but we're not quite there yet." But within twelve to fourteen months, I was able to pay off that old debt. And that's something I'm pretty proud of because it showed me what's possible if I'm diligent and consistent and even maybe a little ferocious about it.

I attribute a lot of that success to my education through reading a ton of books on money and also those affirmations. The brain can't really tell the difference between an actual repetition and an imaginary repetition. Just like when Olympic athletes visualize their ski runs or gymnastics routines, the more you think through a process or think over a certain idea, the more your brain thinks that it is reality and adjusts behavior accordingly. And that's what happened in my life. The more I smashed into my subconscious that I was good with money and was getting better with money, the more my brain tricked my body into behaving that way.

Exercise: Affirmations

I want you to take a few minutes and write down some affirmations dealing specifically with your wealth or your relationship with money. Bear in mind that these should be affirmations, which means they should be positive in nature. Don't write down things like *"I'm not broke anymore,"* or *"I'm not struggling,"* or *"I'm not stressed out over money."* Rather, state these things in the affirmative and write: *"I'm financially free," "I navigate my finances with ease,"* or *"I am calm and at peace when thinking about money."* Notice the difference between stating a desired outcome in the negative versus the affirmative? Make that distinction, and as you write your affirmations, make sure they are indeed in the affirmative.

Some other examples might be saying, "I'm able to do all the things I want to because my bank account allows for it," "I pay all of my bills on time, and I take joy in doing so because I'm responsible with money," or "I'm great with money, and I love the feeling it gives me." Once you complete this exercise, begin reading these affirmations out loud to yourself daily. It'll feel weird at first, but it's an important part of changing your mindset and relationship with money.

Recommended Reading

Think and Grow Rich by Napoleon Hill
Unscripted by MJ DeMarco

CHAPTER 8

How to Make It Happen

"Then what makes a beautiful human being? Isn't it the presence of human excellence? Young friend, if you wish to be beautiful, then work diligently at human excellence. And what is that? Observe those whom you praise without prejudice. The just or the unjust? The just. The even-tempered or the undisciplined? The even-tempered. The self-controlled or the uncontrolled? The self-controlled. In making yourself that kind of person, you will become beautiful—but to the extent you ignore these qualities, you'll be ugly, even if you use every trick in the book to appear beautiful."

–Epictetus, Discourses, 3.1.6b-9[22]

It's All Over but the Crying

This may be the most boring chapter of this whole book because it's the practical exercise, the practical steps to move forward and implement the game plan to start achieving all the things you want. In an earlier chapter, we talked about establishing that identity, and I think that's incredibly vital. If you haven't done that exercise of creating an identity for yourself, begin there. The next step, and what I teach all of my clients, comes after you figure out exactly who you want to be. We have to figure out what you want to achieve. I use a system that I'm sure somebody way smarter than me developed: the

---

[22] Holiday, Ryan, and Stephen Hanselman, *The Daily Stoic: 366 Meditations on Wisdom, Perseverance, and the Art of Living*, 140.

SMART goal system. The letters in the SMART acronym stand for Specific, Measurable, Attainable, Relevant, and Time-bound.

Specific and Measurable are pretty self-explanatory. As you're moving toward a goal, you want to have something very specific in mind, and I'll discuss why in a little bit. You also need something that's measurable so that you can actually track your progress. As far as Attainable is concerned, Bill Gates said, "Most people overestimate what they can do in one year and underestimate what they can do in ten years."[23] So I tell folks I work with to aim really, really big for their five-year goals.

Having said that, I know I'm never going to play in the NBA. First, because I'm not very good at basketball, and second, I don't particularly care for basketball. In viewing your long-term goals and trying to come up with something big that gets you excited and maybe even scares you a little bit, you must hold onto an element of reality. But I can help you with trying to ride that fine line., The R in SMART stands for Relevant. This ties directly back to the identity that you should have come up with in each area of your life. And then we have Time-Bound. I think five years is kind of the sweet spot, so I typically encourage people to shoot for five years.

Again, sometimes, we try to pack too much into 365 days, and we get frustrated when it doesn't come to be. And ten years feels almost ethereal and hard to grasp. I've found five years is close enough that it can keep you motivated but far enough away that you've got some time to build some momentum.

I think I've mentioned this before, but the brain is an interesting machine. It's always working to keep us alive and solve problems. Whatever problem you present to it, that's what it's going to try to solve. So if you give it a very vague or ambiguous problem—for example, say your physical SMART goal at the end of five years was "I want to be healthy"—your brain starts to figure out how to do that. Your brain is creative, and it has the ability

---

[23] *A quote by Bill Gates* (n.d.), https://www.goodreads.com/quotes/302999-most-people-overestimate-what-they-can-do-in-one-year.

to dig deep, but because it can come up with a relatively easy solution to "I want to be healthier," it will probably give you solutions like eating better and exercising. That'll do it, but it's not a very good game plan. And it's not a good game plan because it didn't have a very difficult problem to solve.

This is why it's important to get specific. Instead of your long-term goal being, "In five years, I want to be healthier," make it something like, "In five years, I want to be able to compete in an Ironman, and I want to have a body fat index of 10 to 12 percent. I want to have a resting heart rate of fifty beats per minute. I want a VO2 max of seventy-five milliliters of oxygen per kilogram of body weight per minute. I want to be able to bench 315 pounds, squat 405 pounds, and deadlift 550 pounds." If you're very specific with the goal, it presents the brain with a very specific problem to solve. And then the brain immediately starts to find solutions. So, as opposed to just saying, "I want to be healthier in five years," say something like, "I want to compete in a triathlon or an Ironman competition." The brain will then tell you what you should do.

In this case, you'd need to begin training with cardio and swimming, and you'd have to get a bike. You'd have to plan out weekly massages to help your muscles recover. You should probably track your sleep to be sure you're sleeping appropriately. And you'd also have to dial in your nutrition and consume significantly more calories if you're exercising more consistently. That's what the brain does. It takes a very specific goal and then immediately starts thinking about all the things that need to happen to achieve that goal. So, as you're breaking down your SMART goals, get very specific and make sure that you have the means to measure progress so you know you're staying on track and that your goals are attainable and relevant and tied directly back to the identity you've come up with.

Exercise: SMART Goals

You guessed it. We're going to set up SMART goals now. In the following areas, establish a goal you want to begin striving for. A lot can happen in five years, so aim *big*! There's plenty of opportunity to create some "psychological momentum" and develop a real compound interest of effort. Make sure your goals follow the SMART guideline: **Specific, Measurable, Attainable, Relevant,** and **Time-Bound**. Come up with at least one goal for each category. Here are some examples:

Mental: Within the next five years, I will obtain a master's degree in marketing from an accredited university, which will enhance my skills and knowledge and qualify me for a higher-level job in my current company.

Emotional: Within five years, I will attend five week-long meditation retreats and develop a daily mindfulness practice to manage stress and increase emotional well-being.

Physical: Within five years, I will complete an Olympic distance triathlon in under three hours.

Social: Within five years, I will build a strong support network by cultivating and maintaining positive relationships with at least ten close friends and family members I regularly connect with and support, and who reciprocate that support.

Financial: Within five years, I will pay off all of my credit card debt, build an emergency fund, and establish a long-term savings plan to reach my financial goals, which include putting a down payment on my first investment property.

Mental:

_____

_____

_____

Emotional:

_____

_____

_____

Physical:

_____

_____

_____

Social:

_____

_____

_____

Financial:

_____

_____

_____

Ambushes and Raids

When I was going through the Special Forces qualification course, there was a block of instruction known as "small unit tactics" (SUT). It was really all about planning and also about being miserable. The weather sucked, and we were yelled at a lot, and we had to do miserable things like carrying incredibly heavy rucksacks through the woods with very little sleep or food.

Anyway, the planning portion of SUT taught me how to "backward plan," and I'm going to try to teach you here in the next paragraph or so. "Backward planning" is really just understanding what the desired end state is and then figuring out all the steps leading up to that desired end state. In SUT, if the desired end state was to free the hostages at 1 a.m. or conduct an ambush at 3 a.m. at a certain location on the map, then that's what needed to happen. It was a hard deadline that needed to be met. What led up to the appropriate execution of the mission? Some of the steps might have included deciding whether to travel on foot or by vehicle, determining everyone's roles, checking equipment, making sure everybody was well-fed and properly fueled for the mission, and having a backup plan in case a vehicle broke down.

As you can see, it got super detailed, which was a good thing because everybody knew exactly what their job was and what was expected of them throughout the whole process. In addition, you also had to be aware of your neighbor's job so that if something were to happen and they needed somebody to cover their responsibility, you could step in and do it.

Planning is important because it gives you a very clear path toward the desired end state or objective. And that's an excellent thing. Having said that, I think the main point to planning was to provide a very clear path to the desired end state. We knew what to do if things didn't quite go according to plan. If things deviated from the plan, we knew how to get back on track because we knew every step at each phase of the mission.

The next phase is the most boring part of the whole process. Take your five-year goals and start dividing them up into yearly, monthly, weekly, and daily milestones. The milestones are really just a means by which you can measure the progress you're making and tell whether you're progressing at the rate you should be. If you take a really big goal and look at it on a daily level, it's very small and manageable, and it's something you can do consistently. That's kind of what we're shooting for. You want to be able to develop the habits and perform the tasks in such a way that they can be done consistently without fear of burnout. So again, if your goal is to be competitive in the Ironman sphere, break that down over five years to make it attainable and manageable.

Okay, so if you know what needs to be achieved in five years, what does that look like in the first twelve months? In the first year? Maybe the first year is really just about getting the basics and fundamentals down. Then you break it down a little further. Okay, if that's what you need to get done this first year, what has to happen in the first month? Maybe the first month, you sign up for a membership at the pool and start swimming. And maybe you start shopping for a used bike to begin with. Something that can start getting you out on the road so you can save up for a really nice bike for competition.

All right, so that's the first month. What has to happen the first week? Go swimming two times this week and run three times. If you found an inexpensive bike listed on Craigslist, go for a bike ride. And then break that down even further—what has to happen today? Well, you need to get eight hours of sleep. You need to eat a certain amount of calories broken up into a certain number of meals. And maybe today is your running day, so it might be good to run one mile just to understand what it feels like. So, that's how you break it down. Break it down into such small steps that it's something you can take a bite out of without fear.

Now, there are certain goals that are difficult to quantify and measure. For example, the identity I'm striving for is to be the calmest man in the room. But how do I measure that? If my desired end state is difficult to measure, I can set up systems and practices in my life and measure their regularity. For example, if I want to be the calmest man in the room in five years, the practices that might lead me there would be a daily meditation practice and a daily journal reflective practice. I could also engage in the pause, breathe, think, respond technique before responding in certain situations and keep track of the number of outbursts I may have, trying to decrease those throughout the course of the plan. Even if I can't measure or quantify the desired end state, I can measure all the practices that lead me there, and that's what I recommend to most of my clients.

Being a Nerd is Cool

Another tool I've begun using is a spreadsheet. Going back to the nerd in me, I like looking at numbers and data. It's pretty cool because what it does is lay out my week for me. So, Sunday through Saturday, I can look at the week and allocate certain tasks or activities to be done throughout the week. I break life down into five different categories: mental, physical, emotional, social, and financial. Each one of those could have subcategories, but I think they are the heavy hitters, so I try to focus on those. So maybe I want to read fifteen minutes a day. In the mental category on this spreadsheet, I add fifteen minutes of reading Sunday through Saturday. Maybe in my emotional category, I want to meditate three times a week, so I'll plan it out on my spreadsheet for Monday, Wednesday, and Friday. In the social category, I might add one father-daughter date per week. And then call two friends throughout the week, so that's three things. Go through each category and allocate time for certain activities. Some activities will be a daily thing, and some might be once a week. It kind of depends on what you need and what best suits you. The spreadsheet lets me highlight the things I accomplish as the days progress. If something doesn't get accomplished, I can make a note, and at the end of the week, I can calculate and tally the percentage of execution. I got this idea from the book *12-Week Year* by Brian Moran. Excellent read if you haven't read it already. The goal is to strive for 85 percent or better at the end of the week.[24]

---

[24] Moran, B. P. & Lennington, M., *The 12-Week Year: Get More Done in 12 Weeks than Others Do in 12 Months* (John Wiley & Sons, 2013).

If you're shooting for 85 percent or better, it gets you out of a pass-fail mentality of *I have to do it 100 percent*, or *I'm a complete loser*. We have to understand that life happens sometimes, and it will disrupt your routine. I found that it's typically when you try to dial in your routine that life happens the most. But if you understand that sometimes things will be disrupted and give yourself a little bit of grace, you can look at the end of the week and say it might not have been 100 percent, but it was at least 85 percent. You know you're progressing forward, and you can be happy with that. Because in the grand scheme of things, we are essentially marathon runners for our long-term goals. We're not trying to accomplish this in the next ninety days. We're trying to be consistent over the course of five years to really make some massive gains because consistency over a long time is where you really make your money. After you've calculated your percentages at the end of the week, you can look at your week and troubleshoot your problem areas.

I'll tell you a cool story about why it's important to keep track of this kind of data. Part of my routine was to do some kind of high-intensity interval training (HIIT) workout daily. Because I was collecting all of this data on a daily and weekly basis, I found that on the days I did my HIIT workout first thing in the morning as soon as I woke up, everything else on my list got done. But on the days when I put off that HIIT workout until the afternoon or evening, there were a couple of things that would fall off my schedule and didn't get done. After a few weeks of that pattern, I realized there was a correlation, and I thought, *Why don't I just always do my HIIT workout first?* And so that's what I did. Even though it might have been a psychological thing, I moved it so it was the first thing on my schedule for the day. I got up, did that difficult thing first, and the rest of the stuff just kind of happened because I was ready to go. Because I was able to recognize that based on the data I had collected, I could optimize my schedule to better ensure success over the long haul. So that's another reason why I think it's super important to keep track of all that data.

Below is an example of how I set up a spreadsheet to track my daily habits and actions. The different categories I'm trying to track are in the left-hand column, and the days of the week are across the top row. Down every column, I can see the tasks that need to be done that day. Across every row, I can see all the tasks I have planned out in order to keep me on track for my ultimate goal. Not every category has a task for each day, and that's fine. All that means is there is less room for error if you're striving for an 85 percent execution rate at the end of the week.

As each task is completed, you can fill them in with a color-coded system. On the days when a task was designated but wasn't colored in, that task didn't get done. As you can see, in some of the cells, there are no activities listed, meaning there are no activities planned for that day in that category. The more you track your progress, the more you begin to see what setup works for you. In the early stages of this journey, it will require patience on your part. You may not have things planned out optimally. As you progress and adjust things, you'll be able to dial in.

Table 1								
March 28th-April 3rd	Monday	Tuesday	Wednesday	Thursday	Friday	Saturday	Sunday	% Achieved
Mental	Write for 15 min	Write for 15 min	Write for 15 min	Write for 15 min	Write for 15 min	Write for 15 min	Write for 15 min	86%
	Read for 15 min	Read for 15 min	Read for 15 min	Read for 15 min	Read for 15 min	Read for 15 min	Read for 15 min	71%
	School	School	School	School	School			100%
Physical	Train	Train	Train	Train	Train	Train	Train	86%
	8 min HIIT	8 min HIIT	8 min HIIT	8 min HIIT	8 min HIIT	8 min HIIT	8 min HIIT	100%
Emotional	15 min meditation	15 min meditation	15 min meditation	15 min meditation	15 min meditation	15 min meditation	15 min meditation	71%
Social	Network with clients	Network with colleagues						100%
Financial	10% of paycheck in investments				10% of paycheck in savings			100%

Push the Envelope... When the Time Is Right

I want to tell you a story of one of my clients. He had really great goals in all areas of his life. What I liked most about him was his primary focus on being a good family man. His goal was, "I want to be a good father, good husband, and ensure that my family is set up for success." He orchestrated his weeks and days to love his family as best as he could, and I thought that was really great. However, as we worked together, we noticed that he consistently hit 100 percent in every single category we tracked on the spreadsheet. Week after week, he was knocking it out of the park, and he was feeling really good about himself. But then I started asking him if there was an area where he could start pushing himself because there was clearly still more in his bucket he could give.

After thinking about it a little bit, he thought he might be able to step it up in the physical area and push his workouts or nutrition, so that's what he did. The only reason I bring this up is to encourage you to start pushing the envelope a little bit if you're consistently hitting 100 percent on everything week after week because it means there's definitely room for you to stretch and grow. Think about the areas in your own life—mental, physical, emotional, social, and financial—where you want to grow the most. Circle those areas and write down how you want to grow and in what way.

The Magic Pill

How do I start implementing all of these ideas in my life today? How do I start to make sure I'm progressing and not becoming complacent? I'm glad you asked. Routine was huge in the military. You wake up at a certain time, you exercise at a certain time, you eat at a certain time, and everybody dresses the same. I joke around when people come to me and say, "Hey, Chris, I think I'm going to join the military. Can you tell me about basic training?" I tell them basic training will be the easiest part of their entire military career because they will have outsourced all the decision-making to other people. You don't have to think. The intent behind basic training is to teach you to follow orders even if you don't exactly understand the *why* behind them.

So when I say you've outsourced all decision-making to other people, I mean that they tell you when to wake up, when to exercise, how to exercise, when to get dressed, how fast to get dressed, when to eat, when to learn, when to rest (which was minimal), and when to shut up and just listen. Every decision that you should be making has been outsourced to your drill sergeants, at least early on in basic training.

Eventually, you get into leadership roles that require you to do some thinking for yourself, so essentially, basic training is the easiest time in your military career because you don't have to make a decision. You just have to listen to what your drill sergeants say and then do exactly what they say and how they say to do it. Okay, so back to routine. Routine is one of the easiest ways to capitalize on your time. Your routine can become your "drill sergeant" for life. You create a plan and a system in your life that you don't have to question. You just do it.

And I'm not talking about the three-hour "morning routine" that you might have seen some YouTube guru describe. A routine should be a well-thought-out plan, and it should be structured so you get the most out of your day. Some super-elaborate morning routine that takes several hours before you start doing anything isn't the goal here. I guess if you're well off enough and can afford to spend three hours doing your "morning routine," that's another thing, but *your* routine should be a schedule you created when you were thinking clearly and wasn't stressed that you can fall back on so you don't burn up too much mental bandwidth trying to figure out what comes next in your day. The point of creating a routine is so you don't have to think about what comes next. You've created an optimal plan that will steadily progress you forward, and then you *follow* the plan.

Example

Here's an example to get your morning going, but keep in mind the routine shouldn't stop in the morning. It should continue throughout the day… every day. That's what makes it a routine. Take this forty-five minute morning routine and expand on it to maximize the rest of your day.

Step one: Wake up forty-five minutes before you normally do.

Step two: Drink 500 ml of water. I put a pinch of salt in mine. (5 min.)

Step three: Do eight to ten minutes of a HIIT workout. I like to jump rope. (10 min.)

Step four: Write at least one sentence in a journal. Doesn't matter what. Just put at least one thought down on paper. (5 min.)

Step five: Meditate for five to ten minutes. If you've never meditated or have trouble with it, dial it back to two minutes or even one minute to start. Download an app if you don't know what to do. (5-10 min.)

Step six: Write down what needs to happen today. Create your to-do list for the day. Put the most important things first. Create a block of time for the stupid tasks like answering emails and stuff. Yes, emails are stupid. (15 min.)

Step seven: Get ready for the day.

Okay, why those steps?

Step one: because being rushed in the morning is stupid. Having plenty of time to deal with stuff is a sign of intelligence and control over one's schedule. Notice I wrote to wake up forty-five minutes before you normally do, not forty-five minutes before you leave for work. I know you can probably get ready in like thirty minutes, and that's fine. Set your alarm clock for forty-five minutes before you normally do, and get up when it goes off.

Step two: because you've been unconscious for almost eight hours. Your body and mind need water to function properly, and they've been deprived of it all night. Hydrate to help your brain and body.

Step three: because doing a little bit of cardio in the morning is good all around, but we do it in the morning for a psychological win first thing in the day. You can ride that momentum till almost lunchtime if you need to.

Step four: because putting thoughts on paper can help you gain perspective on life and can help you recognize patterns and figure out how to capitalize on them or change them. It can help get you out of negative feedback loops in your mind. Sometimes, to help prevent me from spiraling down negative rabbit holes, I'll write those shitty thoughts down. It breaks the feedback loop and allows my mind to focus on other things.

Step five: because meditation becomes a superpower after a while. Learning to stay calm in stressful situations, learning to focus on one task at a time, learning to be present with those around you are all skills that can be developed, and they are developed through meditation. It's a superpower—learn to harness it.

Step six: because you need to be in charge of your day, not react to it. Take control of your schedule, and you'll begin to separate yourself from your peers in a very positive way.

Step seven: because you are now fully prepared to tackle life. Notice this didn't take a long time to accomplish. Routines are in place to streamline your life, not overcomplicate it.

I recommend to a lot of my clients I work with to start creating systems that maximize your time. "Well, Chris, how do I do that?" Having spent ten years in the military, routine becomes everything. Often, there are a lot of troops in a certain area that need to be taken care of. Things have to be pretty time-efficient to maximize the ability to provide rest and nourishment for a large number of people, and the best way to do that is routine. Granted, that's not a very sexy answer when talking about systems in your life. Everybody's kind of looking for that magic pill that will fix everything. "Give me the secret that's going to fix my day and then fix my year and then fix my life."

There is no magic pill.

Rather, it's a list of basic principles that if you apply, and apply regularly, they will do the thing they're intended to do, which is organize your life, streamline and optimize your schedule, and move you toward success in a very intentional and methodical way.

This is sort of the tortoise and the hare situation here. You can try to sprint toward success, but if you go slow and steady, it's a better approach because you can maintain consistency longer. Consistency is where you make your money. We had a phrase in the military: "Slow is smooth. Smooth is fast." Ensuring that you're moving with intention, in a way that minimizes mistakes, missteps, or mishaps, was always the best approach. Intentionally slowing your movements down allows you to think through the steps coming up so as to minimize the need to fix mistakes. Maybe this seems counterintuitive to the sense of urgency I talked about in an earlier chapter regarding the lifetime countdown, but trust me. Taking your time to do something correctly the first time saves you tons of time on the backend because things don't need to be redone.

Set your schedule up in such a way that it's streamlined and efficient. One of the best ways to do that is to regulate when you do things—go to bed at the same time every day, regardless of what day of the week it is, and then wake up at the same time every day, regardless of what day of the week it is. That's the best way to ensure your sleep cycle is regular, scheduled, and ready to go. Have a particular time for reading. Or maybe a specific time for social media and entertainment. If you can set up this schedule, this routine that's done every single day, it begins to happen on autopilot.

Magic Pill Number 2

Another thing I learned from the military is the importance of having checklists. If you think about it, routines are really just a checklist for the hours of your day. This is what I'm going to do. I'm going to wake up at this time. Check. I'm going to eat breakfast. Check. I'm going to work out at this time. Check. I'm going to my job at this time. Check. It's really just a checklist, a to-do list for your day. The beauty of checklists and why I believe in them is that they eliminate second-guessing or overthinking when working through a situation or task. Remember my MARCH acronym? The only reason I bring this up is because when I'm presented with a very stressful, chaotic situation, it removes the second-guessing and overthinking when addressing that situation. I just remember the MARCH sequence and then go to work solving those little problems throughout the situation until I get to the end. And then, I start over and recheck all the things I just did, and hopefully that helps the individual.

I read something very recently in the book *On Target* (Mark Greaney's Gray Man novel series) that was written kind of tongue-in-cheek, but it's appropriate. Greaney wrote: *"A plan is just a big list of shit that's not going to happen."* And I had to laugh because that's often accurate. Throughout the whole planning process, you plan everything down to the most minute detail. But plans have a way of veering off course and changing very quickly because things happen when you're trying to conduct the mission, right? And so the plan should be incredibly structured and well-thought-out and should be able to answer any of the questions you have along the way. But it should also be flexible enough that if you were to deviate from parts of it, it won't break your heart too much because you still have that guide, that path to get you back on track.

In other words, be willing to adapt and adjust. As I mentioned before, five years is a long time. A lot can happen. If you've set up some goals that you're striving for, you might realize, "I don't really want to be a bodybuilder. I want to just be a well-rounded athlete with tons of mobility and flexibility who is able to maneuver in various things and be able to sit on an airplane without having to pay for two seats." It's okay if your goals change. If you have a firm identity and know exactly *who* you want to be, then the adjustment of goals is totally fine because you can find a different, better goal that better aligns with the type of person you're trying to become. So be flexible, and don't beat yourself up too much about switching things up.

I also mentioned in an earlier chapter the Ouroboros, the snake that's eating its own tail. To reiterate, as the snake eats its own tail and destroys and devours the pieces of it that are no longer necessary and no longer serving it, that's where it gets the nourishment and strength to grow and become better during this planning phase. It's important to take a look at and take stock of the things that you're willing to give up to achieve your goals. If you're unwilling to give up anything, then maybe you don't really want the goal. So look at the things you are willing to give up—maybe it's drinking, fast food, or processed foods. Maybe it's people that don't add any value to your life. So, start thinking through that.

And that ties right into avoiding the blood-sucking vampires, which, as we mentioned before, are things that suck your time and energy with very little return for that sacrifice, very little return on that investment. That can look like social media or binge-watching movies or TV on various networks or people. Maybe it's people who just refuse to progress in their own journey and will only hold you back. I know that's a hard conversation to have. A good exercise that might help you is imagining what the enemy's most dangerous course of action is, and then what their most likely course of action is. That was part of our planning process. Keep in mind that you may not have an actual enemy, but there are going to be things that happen in life that try to veer you off course. It's important to anticipate some of that and then have a plan for how you're going to respond to it.

The point of this chapter is to provide you with some insights on how to plan out the next five years of your life so you can achieve all the things you want. The most important part is to know for sure what kind of person you want to become. That's the foundation on which you stack all of your goals and upon which your planning process is rooted. Once you know *who* you want to be, you can figure out where you want to be and what you want to achieve. Set up your SMART goals. Goals are great but require a certain amount of planning to achieve. Spend some time planning out the steps required to achieve your big goals. Once your plan is laid out, develop a routine or daily checklist to streamline this process. You want to eventually be able to tackle the daily tasks required of you on autopilot. Learn to avoid the vampires that try to rob you of your time and energy. And last, track all of your progress. Keep track of how you're doing in all areas so you know where to step it up or how to optimize things. Patterns never lie.

Recommended Reading

The Compound Effect by Darren Hardy

Atomic Habits by James Clear

Conclusion

The path to excellence is not an easy one to follow. It's simple, but it isn't easy. Becoming excellent in whatever it is you choose to pursue really just takes doing the right actions consistently. The tricky part is when life happens—spoiler alert, it always does. Sometimes, you start to get complacent, and your plan gets pushed to the back burner. Sometimes, hell shows up for breakfast and closes doors you were moving toward. In the grand scheme of things, you have very little control over.

The more I examine life, the more I'm convinced the only things we can control are our own thoughts and our own actions. So, make sure you're in charge of those two things. You are in charge of how you approach life. You are in charge of the thoughts you dwell on and the actions you take on a daily basis. You get to decide the direction of your life. Choose not to be influenced by the vampires that show up every day. Choose to be intentional with the type of person you're becoming and take the appropriate actions to achieve it. Choose to be the calmest one in the room. Choose to be the most interesting person you know. Choose to hold yourself and the people around you to a high standard and help them when they don't quite measure up.

Striving for excellence in all areas of your life is a noble pursuit, but it requires you to be *proactive,* not *reactive* to life. Figure out what the right action is and do it. And then do it again. And again. Don't get overwhelmed by the expectations the world has placed on you. Focus on the next step to get you closer to the kind of person you want to become. Excellence isn't a single impressive event that you get to coast on for the rest of your life. Excellence is the accumulation of small actions done consistently. And remember, you're never finished. You're in it for the long haul. It's a lifelong pursuit of the potential you have within you. That should both scare you a little and fill you with excitement. You can't go wrong becoming the best version of yourself.

My hope is you got some value from this book. I definitely don't have all the answers, but the lessons I've learned throughout my life, some of which I've shared here, have helped me progress toward my goals and continue to become the kind of man I want to be. I'll leave links to my social media below just in case you want to hear more of my philosophy.

One final note: if the message you read here resonated with you, and you're looking for some help mapping out your future so that you will feel a sense of contentment when sitting on your rocking chair at ninety years old, contact me at Christopher@toptiergoals.com. Strive for excellence in all things every day. Thank you.

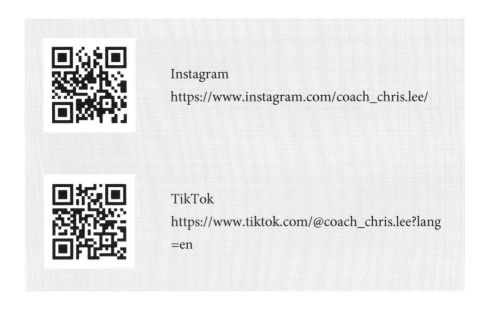

Instagram
https://www.instagram.com/coach_chris.lee/

TikTok
https://www.tiktok.com/@coach_chris.lee?lang=en

Just to say thanks for buying and reading my book, I would like to give you a free welcome call with me, no strings attached!

Calendly https://calendly.com/christopher-douglas-lee/welcome

Additional Reading

Identity:
- *Atlas Shrugged* Ayn Rand
- *The Virtue of Selfishness* – Ayn Rand
- *Wild at Heart* – John Eldredge
- *Becoming Supernatural* – Joe Dispenza

Productivity:
- *Deep Work* – Cal Newport
- *Atomic Habits* – James Clear
- *The Compound Effect* – Darren Hardy
- *12-Week Year* – Brian Moran
- *Objective Secure* – Nick Lavery

Emotional:
- *The Daily Stoic* – Ryan Holiday
- *The Untethered Soul* – Michael Singer
- *The Surrender Experiment* – Michael Singer
- *The Subtle Art of Not Giving a F*ck* – Mark Manson

Social:
- *Never Split the Difference* – Chris Voss
- *The Five Love Languages* – Gary Chapman
- *No More Mr. Nice Guy* – Robert Glover
- *The Setup* – Dan Bilzarian
- *Fire in the Dark* – Jack Donovan

Physical:

High-Intensity Training the Mike Mentzer Way – Mike Mentzer
Any Jack Reacher Novel – Lee Child
On Target by Mark Greaney (Gray Man novel series)

Financial:

Unscripted – MJ Demarco
Money Fastlane – MJ Demarco
Think and Grow Rich – Napoleon Hill
Rich Dad Poor Dad – Robert Kiyosaki
Seven Years to Seven Figures – Michael Masterson
Richest Man in Babylon – George Clason
The Millionaire Next Door – Cotter Smith, Thomas J. Stanley PhD, et al.
Total Money Makeover – Dave Ramsey
How to Be a Billionaire – Martin Fridson
10X – Grant Cardone

THANK YOU FOR READING MY BOOK!

DOWNLOAD YOUR FREE GIFTS

Just to say thanks for buying and reading our book, we would like to give you a free bonus gift, no strings attached!

Scan the QR code:

I appreciate your interest in my book, and value your feedback as it helps me improve future versions of this book. I would appreciate it if you could leave your invaluable review on Amazon.com with your feedback. Thank you!

Made in the USA
Columbia, SC
01 July 2024

8e6e608c-b460-4081-906c-cf7ba4993b84R02